Best of Making

JEWELRY

QUARRY BOOKS

Gloucester, Massachusetts

First published in the United States of America by:
Quarry Books, an imprint of
Rockport Publishers, Inc.
33 Commercial Street
Gloucester, Massachusetts 01930-5089
Telephone: (508) 282-9590
Fax: (508) 283-2742

ISBN 1-56496-429-9

10 9 8 7 6 5 4 3 2 1

Designer: Laura Herrmann Design

Printed in Hong Kong
by Midas Printing Limited.

CONTENTS

JEWELRY BASICS

You don't have to be a highly skilled professional to create beautiful jewelry. With just a little imagination and the right materials and tools, you can produce wonderful works of art from classic jewelry elements such as beads, precious metals, and stones. Or you can transform mundane, household items such as buttons, fabric scraps, and newspapers into sophisticated jewelry. To produce fabulous designs with a professional finish, you will need the findings, tools, and techniques that join, link, and make up your jewelry.

Materials

Beads have been used in jewelry making since the beginning of time, but they can be expensive to buy in large quantities. Many of the projects in this book show you how to make your own beads using materials such as modeling clay and paper. Pick up other materials at yard sales and antique fairs. Never throw out a broken necklace or bracelet—the remaining beads and clasps can always be worked into other designs.

Synthetic polymer clays can be used to make spectacular beads and bases in every shape imaginable. Fired in a low-temperature domestic oven and then varnished, polymer clays can imitate some of the finest ceramics. Take advantage of the wide selection of decorative paper available and add a colorful, patterned finishing layer to a plain papier-mâché base. Roll strips of colorful paper to make beads of different shapes and lengths.

Almost all jewelry making requires the use of findings, which is the jeweler's term for the basic components that give your design a neat finish and help each piece hang correctly. They should be the right size for your design; if they are in proportion to the material that you choose for your jewelry, they will help balance the overall design. All findings are readily available in craft stores, from bead suppliers, and even in department stores. You can buy them in precious or nonprecious metals.

You will also need the right bases in your craft box to make fabulous hair ornaments. Metal clip-fastening bases and plain white plastic headbands are available ready to decorate from craft or jewelry suppliers. You can also use inexpensive clips, combs, and headbands from the local drugstore.

Findings

CLASPS usually consist of two pieces that join together to secure your jewelry. They come in an assortment of designs, including the screw clasps and S-clasps. You can also buy decorative two-part clasps that have preformed holes for more than one thread. Choose a style that suits your design.

CALOTTE CRIMPS conceal and secure knots at both ends of a necklace or bracelet and help make the jewelry look polished. Calotte crimps come in different sizes to suit the thread you are using; round calottes can open sideways or from the top; square calottes are ideal for thicker threads and for clamping unusual material such as feathers.

JUMP RINGS are circular or oval metal rings that are not completely joined together. They come in a variety of sizes and thicknesses to suit all kinds of jewelry projects. Use them to link two findings together.

JEWELER'S WIRE is available in gold, silver, copper, or plated metals and in several different gauges. Wire is easy to coil and work into intricate shapes and decorative spirals. The finer the gauge, the easier it is to work with, but choose a thickness to suit the beads and the overall design. You can use wire to make your own hat and lapel pins by using a metal file to sharpen the ends into a point. Wire is also useful when head and eye pins are not long enough or are too thick to pass through tiny beads.

Other Findings

Other useful findings for making jewelry are ornate END SPACERS and HANGERS, which often have two, three, or five preformed holes on one side and a single loop on the other. End spacer bars can be used to make multistrand designs and to attach the clasp to the start and finish of a necklace or bracelet. Large BELL CAPS are decorative caps added to each end of a necklace or bracelet to conceal a collection of knots. Join PENDANT CLASPS to jump rings to make a pendant or charm hang correctly, or directly clamp onto fabric to seed charms.

PIN BACKS are essential for a professional finish and come in a choice of metal finishes. Flat bar backs have pierced holes along their length, and are available in circular or oval shapes in retail stores. You can buy special perforated fittings with claws that clamp over a corresponding base and these can be used to sew beads or fabric designs to. Stick pins come in a variety of lengths and have a blunt head and pointed end that should be inserted into a protective cap. Other variations come with a flat disc set at the top. A head pin is like a blunt-ended dressmaker's pin that is particularly useful for making charms. Eye pins have a preformed loop at one end and are most often used to link beads or findings together but can also be used to make beaded bar pins.

EARRING FITTINGS come in all shapes and sizes, for both pierced and unpierced ears. Hoops, clip earrings, post earrings, and hooks are the most common earring styles. They are also available with ornate designs, or with one or more integral loops or holes to hang more than one drop.

HAIR CLIPS from jewelry suppliers come in a selection of sizes — the smaller ones can be used to hold sections of hair in place while the larger ones will secure a ponytail or chignon. Hair combs and headbands are available with plain or intricately designed tops and come in a variety of sizes to suit different styles and thicknesses of hair. Hair slides are easy to make using fabric scrapes, polymer clays, and fine sheet metals. Make your own pins from wooden skewers or look for more original ideas like brightly-colored plastic needles, knitting row markers and cable needles, or thick jeweler's wire wrought into shape.

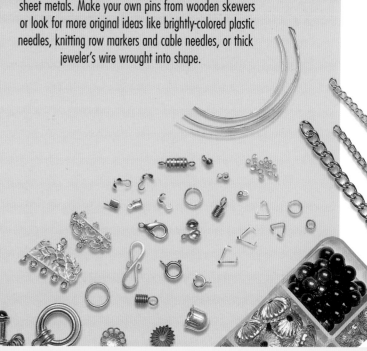

All of the projects in this book are easy to make and require little space for their creation—most can be put together at the kitchen table with only the basic tools. Lay down a craft board to protect the table from damage, and provide a flat, even surface to work on. A self-healing cutting mat, marked with ruled lines, makes it easy to draw and cut shapes and is useful for working with metal. Organize your bases and decorative elements in boxes and trays.

Small round-nosed and needle-nosed pliers, available at jewelry and bead suppliers, make opening, closing, and linking together findings much easier. Use two pairs of pliers to open and close jump rings. Buy them with integral wire cutters or invest in a separate pair of wire cutters for trimming head and eye pins, and jeweler's wire.

Use a craft knife for making precise cuts and tin cutters for cutting metals. For measuring and cutting perfect straight lines, a steel ruler is more practical than plastic as it won't be damaged by a craft knife. A tape measure is essential for measuring curved surfaces.

Other useful tools include a blunt needle, a fine bradawl, and a single hole punch for making holes in hard materials. Use toothpicks or basic wooden kebab skewers for softer materials like polymer clays. Tweezers and toothpicks help to hold and glue small jewels and beads in place. Attach a small clamp or clothespin to hold items together while the glue sets. Metal files are useful if you prefer working with sheet tin, copper, or pewter, but are not essential for other materials where the rougher side of an emery board will work just as well.

Tips

Lightly scuff plastic surfaces with an emery board before gluing to provide a surface the object can adhere to. Make sure surfaces are dust-free before gluing. Use just as much glue as you need for each project—too much glue will cause it to ooze out, and too little glue will create a weak bond.

Stringing & Knotting

Stringing beads onto thread is a simple way to make jewelry. Before you begin, decide how long you want the piece to be. To calculate the total number of beads you will need, count how many beads fit into 1 inch / 2.5 cm, then multiply this by the length required.

Silk and cotton thread both hang well and can be color-coordinated to the beads, but they are not very strong. Use several strands together if you are working with heavy beads.

To prevent them from getting tangled, run them through a beeswax cake. Or try polyester thread already coated with beeswax. If you prefer the drape of the silk and cotton threads, knot between every bead or small group of beads to prevent the beads from tumbling in all directions if the thread breaks. A needle is helpful when you are drawing the knot up close to a bead. Make sure the knot is large enough to resist slipping through the bead hole.

When making necklaces and bracelets with a central point of interest, thread both ends of the thread with a needle and work from the middle outward on both threads at the same time, keeping the design symmetrical. Another advantage of working from the center is that the length can be adjusted by adding or taking away beads at each end—you won't have to start all over again.

Fine, invisible thread, though not very strong, is useful for tiny lightweight beads like rocailles because it can be threaded through a beading needle. Nylon line and tiger tail are more substantial and will support most designs. They are both almost invisible to the eye and can be used without a needle. Nylon is inexpensive and easy to handle, but will not always hang well, so it is best for fun bead necklaces.

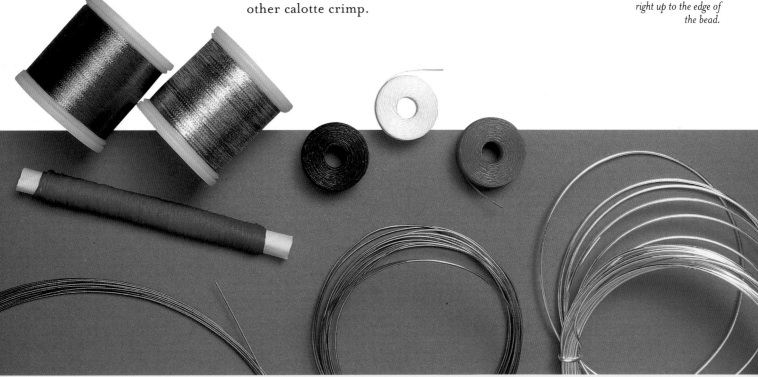

Tiger tail is a good, all-purpose jeweler's thread. It is easy to make starter knots in tiger tail, though sometimes you need pliers to pull it tight, or you can make a loop and secure it with a crimp bead. Leather thong, decorative cord, string, and even raffia can also be used. Thong is good for stringing individual beads, small groups of beads, or objects with large holes. String and raffia can be used to complement more unusual material, such as shells.

How you knot and finish your piece depends on the length you choose. You can string on the beads and simply knot the two ends together, add a blob of superglue to secure the knot and hide it inside a bead. Or knot one end and secure in a calotte crimp (see Findings), string on the beads, and then knot and secure the other end to another calotte crimp.

Use a needle to knot right up to the edge of the bead.

Linking Beads

There are many other ways to make jewelry besides using bead strands. Link together groups of beads in similar colors with head or eye pins to hang as charms. You can wire each bead individually, which is quite time consuming but produces an expensive-looking finish, or work the beads in small groups. To make the beads go further and use up leftover beads, insert short lengths of chain between each group of beads.

To make charms, use a finding called a head pin, which is like a blunt, flexible sewing pin with a flat "head" at one end. The flat head prevents the beads from sliding off, if the head pin slips through the bead hole, add a small stopper bead first. Slide the beads onto the pin in the order you want, trim the wire with wire cutters if necessary, and then turn a loop with round-nosed pliers. The loop can then be attached to a bead necklace with a jump ring or opened slightly and joined directly to a chain.

Eye pins are ideal for linking beads together because they already have performed loop in one end.

Use short pins for single beads and longer ones for groups of beads. Slide the beads onto each pin, trim the wire, and turn a loop, just as you would with a head pin. To link the beads together, use jump rings or open up a loop on the pin and join to the next loop. To make charms, you will need to turn a small spiral in the end with round-nosed pliers. You can then leave this protruding as a decorative effect or turn it under so the bottom bead sits on it. For linking beads, simply turn a loop in each end with pliers.

Multistrand & Multidrop Jewelry

To create more elaborate necklaces, bracelets, and earrings, work with multiple strands and add special clasps and other decorative findings to make the jewelry look polished. Multistrand necklaces and bracelets can simply be several bead strands joined to one another or to an ornate spacer bar. More elaborate designs can be worked on more than one thread, split and worked individually, then brought back together.

To make the most basic multistrand necklace and bracelet and multidrop earrings, bead lots of strands of similar lengths. Finish the ends with calotte crimps and link the loops of these together in a jump ring. The ends can then be disguised with a pretty bell cap (see Finishing Techniques). To use end spacer bars, select one with the same number of holes as the number of threads you are using—usually two, three, or five—finish each beaded strand with a calotte crimp, and join them directly or with jump rings to holes on the bar.

For a more sophisticated multistrand look, work on two or more threads, stringing beads onto all three threads for part of the design and individual threads at other points. With this style, it is important to work out your design first and to keep both sides of the design symmetrical. More textured effects can be achieved if you twist or braid the threads when they are worked on separately.

Basic Metalwork

Working with sheet metal creates a new world of design possibilities and is not as daunting as it seems—you don't need to have special skills or an expensive set of tools to create fabulous results.

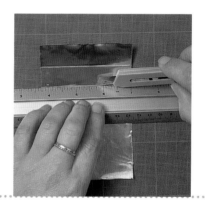

Craft suppliers stock tin, aluminum, copper, and pewter in sheet form, which is easily cut and shaped using heavy duty scissors, tin cutters, or a craft knife. You can recycle materials such as soda cans as another alternative; make sure these are washed thoroughly and dried carefully to prevent rusting before starting your project.

Pressing a blunt needle, knitting needle, or ballpoint pen onto the metal will mark the outline of the shape to be cut. A self-healing rubber cutting mat is useful to work on as it keeps the metal from slipping as you mark the shape, and its surface has enough "give" to allow you to indent the metal easily.

(Use a wad of newspaper if you don't have a cutting mat.)

Other metalwork tools include fine hand files suitable for metal, a hammer and panel pin for creating pierced designs, and a steel ruler for marking straight lines.

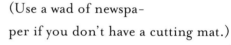

To create relief patterns, make a tracing of your design and tape it over the metal shape. Work on a self-healing cutting mat or wad of newspapers, and use a tip of a knitting needle to trace the design onto the metal, pressing down firmly. Use a smooth action to create the best finish—stopping and starting in the middle of a line can create distortion. Wrap a piece of tape close to the end of the knitting needle to help prevent your fingers from slipping.

Pierced designs are easy to master and provide scope for creating a wide variety of different motifs. Draw your motif on paper and lay a piece of tracing paper on top. Transfer the design to the tracing paper by marking a dotted outline in pencil, making sure the dots are evenly spaced. Tape this to the metal and use the tip of a needle to make light indentations where the dots are to be placed. Remove the tracing paper and then use a hammer and panel pin to pierce the detail.

Textured finishes add a different dimension to designs and are easy to work on most soft metals. For a hammered look, you can use anything from the end of a paintbrush to a more professional ball-headed hammer. To prevent scratching the metal, wrap the head of the hammer with a piece of felt. Working on a different surface can also create varied finishes, so experiment first on metal scraps.

Polish the metal gently with a soft cloth to remove any greasy finger marks. Take care not to press too hard on relief designs as this can spoil the raised effect. File sharp edges smooth using a fine metal file or emery board. Backing the finished design with stiff cardboard, suede, or leather will give it more substance.

Safety Note

Use protective gloves and goggles when working with metal as the edges can be very sharp, and bits can fly off when cutting.

Finishing Techniques

How you finish your jewelry can make or break your designs. To get a truly professional look, use findings. Jump rings link together two or more pieces so they hang freely. To keep the shape of the ring, and to ensure that the two ends meet perfectly again, open the rings at the joint using pliers, twisting the ends away from each other sideways. To close, simply twist the ends back again so that they meet exactly.

Hold a jump ring with two pairs of pliers positioned at either side of the joint. Gently twist the ends away from each other sideways to open, and twist back again to close.

End knots can look ugly and need to be disguised. For single-strand jewelry, a calotte crimp is usually sufficient; its preformed loop can be joined to a jump ring and clasp.

There are several type of calottes to choose from. Round calottes are hinged either at the side or bottom and have a gap for the thread to pass through. For sideways-opening calottes, position the knot in the "cup" of one half and use needle-nosed pliers to squeeze the two sides together.

Place the knot at the end of a length of thread in the cup of a calotte crimp and squeeze the two halves together using needle-nosed pliers.

Make sure the thread is going in the right direction before you secure the crimp. If you are using calottes that open from the loop end, you will need to pass the thread through a small gap in the hinged end before knotting, then close in the same way as before. Use square calottes for thick cord or thong; they are open on one side, which is where you insert the thread. With needle-nosed pliers, fold one side over the thread and then the other side to secure.

Use calottes on multistrand necklaces and bracelets when you are attaching a decorative end spacer, but if the design has lots of strands, add a bell cap to hide the calottes.

For this different style of calotte crimp, the thread is pushed through a hole in the base of the crimp before knotting. The two halves are then squeezed together.

These tiny crimp beads are used most often when working with tiger tail and are squeezed tightly with flat-nosed pliers to secure the loop in the tiger tail.

Slip the loops of the calottes onto a jump ring, but before closing the ring, push it through the loop of an eye pin. Insert the pin through hole in the cap, trim it to about 3/8 inch/1 cm with wire cutters and turn a loop with round-nosed pliers.

Once you have successfully concealed the knot, complete the jewelry with a clasp. Choose a style to suit your design: screw clasps and spring rings are the simplest and most discreet in appearance. Two-part clasps are often more decorative and they have more than one hole, which makes them ideal for multistrand jewelry. To attach a clasp, open up a jump ring and slip it through the loop on the calotte and the hole in the clasp, then close the ring. Two-part clasps have a corresponding catch, but for a spring-ring clasp, you

A bell cap conceals a collection of knots or just adds a decorative end to a necklace. Slip the open eye of an eye pin through a calotte loop in the tiger tail. Close it securely. Push the pin through the central hole in the cap, and trim and turn a loop in the opposite end.

will need to attach a jump ring to the other end to complete the clasp.

To finish a basic pin, make sure the bar or disc back is the right size to support the design and is positioned in the correct place to ensure the pin sits correctly or it will fall forward when worn. It is easy to check this by temporarily fixing the finding in place with Blu Tak or plasticine. Use long stick pins for hat pins and shorter ones for lapel pins. If you can't find the right length, make you own stick pins from jeweler's wire.

A necklace clasp adds the perfect finishing touch to a necklace. To attach, simply insert an open jump ring through the loop at the end of the thread (or the loop of a calotte crimp) and through the loop on the clasp at the same time.

BASES FOR BARRETTES & PINS

SIMPLE FLAT-BACKED BASES FOR HAIR clips, hair slides, and pins are easy to make from polymer and air dry clays, papier-mâché shapes, and fabric scraps. These can then be decorated with paint effects, dazzling bead detail, or simple embroidery.

Safety Note

The simplest bases can be shaped from polymer clays. You can use cookie cutters or, with a cardboard template of your own design, cut out the shape carefully using a craft knife. For a three-dimensional effect, layer clay shapes on top of each other. Press them with objects such as a perforated fitting or fallen leaves to create a textured finish. Design a glittering jewel-encrusted finish by pressing glass beads or flat-backed jewel stones into the surface—glass will not melt when the clay is fired. If you are working with several colors, be careful to keep your hands clean to avoid mixing the colors. Use acrylic paints or jewel stones to disguise any faults (water-based colors separate on the polymer base).

Cardboard shapes layered with pasted strips of newspaper, a basic papier-mâché technique, can also become simple bases perfect for painting and decorating with fabric scraps, braids, or sequins. Create textured finishes by gluing string or paper pulp in pretty patterns to the base shape, or add jewel stones for a touch of glamour.

Decorate these bases with beads, charms, or drops by inserting eye pins or piercing holes at the relevant points. Hang just one beautiful jewel from the center bottom of the design or dangle several beaded strands. To attach such findings, trim an eye pin to size (approximately 1/4 to 3/8 inch / .5 cm to 1 cm, depending on the size of the design) and insert it into the edge of a clay or papier-mâché design before it is set. Dab a bit of glue to secure it once it is rigid. Then join wired single beads or groups of beads directly or with a jump ring to the eye pin.

Decorative necklace clasps can also be turned into instant pins by separating the two parts, discarding the plain section, and gluing a pin back to the reverse side. These are often very ornate and can be set with pearls, jewel stones, and diamante. Use the attached loop to hang stunning beads or other charms. You can also adapt large flat, doughnut-style beads typically used as pendants. By looking past the obvious, you can find all sorts of ingenious alternatives.

17

DECORATIVE EFFECTS

Beads are ideal for creating unique decorative effects. Look for smaller beads, which are more suited for embroidery work than for making necklaces. Use them to highlight patterns on decorative braids or to add a glittering finish to ribbon-wrapped combs and bands.

Jewel stones add instant glamour to most pieces of jewelry. Buy them with flat backs, which are easy to glue in position, or cut like genuine precious stones, which must be set in special metal mounts. These stones are made from acrylic or glass and come in a range of sizes, some with holes to allow them to be sewn in place. Both types have mirrored backs and care needs to be taken when handling them as the mirror finish can easily be scratched and spoil the finished effect.

Sequins come in an abundant array of sizes, colors, and shapes and can be sewn or glued directly to any type of hair accessory. Specialist craft and jewelry suppliers include most shapes in their catalogues; some even offer cheap bags of "sweepings"—sequins literally swept from the floor, cleaned, and bagged.

Synthetic polymer clay comes in a fantastic range of colors that can be used on their own, or several different colors twisted together to create wonderful marbled effects. Once kneaded to soften and remove air bubbles, they can be rolled out like pastry and cut and shaped with a craft knife. Work intricate patterns into their surface by carefully adding different colored clays.

Paint plain bases with subtle metallic paints to resemble precious metals.

Papier-mâché is one of the most versatile modeling mediums for any form of craft work and jewelry design is no exception. Using the most basic techniques you can cover simple cardboard shapes with newspaper.

Found objects can be used to make fun, innovative hair jewelry and frequently cost nothing at all.

Scraps of fabric, and embroidery threads are easy to transform into stylish designs. More unusual materials can be picked up on a visit to a flea market, rummage sale, or antique fair—old watches, broken up, can be used as decorations and to transform something ordinary into a fun, unique design.

Transform unexciting hair accessories into something special by covering them with luxurious ribbons, rich textured braids, or colorful embroidery threads. These can be simply wrapped along the length of a headband or top of a hair comb—color coordinate one with a special outfit. To hold the ribbon or braid in place securely, place a blob of glue on the wrong side of a headband or comb close to one end, and position the thread or braid over the glue and hold in place while it dries using a small clamp or a clothespin. Finish the same way at the opposite end.

BEAD IDEAS

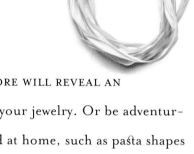

A VISIT TO YOUR LOCAL CRAFTS STORE WILL REVEAL AN array of beads to use in making your jewelry. Or be adventurous and use objects you can find at home, such as pasta shapes or feathers from a feather duster, to substitute for beads. If you choose to make your own beads, try unusual materials, such as newspaper and magazine cuttings, colored foil, or fabric scraps.

Clay Beads

One of the most effective materials to use is polymer clay. It is available in a fantastic range of colors, molds easily, and sets hard in a low-temperature oven. There are several comparable brands available, each with their own malleability, baking time, and color selection.

Plain beads in a single color can be molded into any shape you want and then decorated with acrylic paints (water-based paints don't cover as well). To make the beads, first knead the clay until it is soft and pliable, then roll it out into a log shape, ¼ to ¾ inch / .5 to 2 cm in diameter, depending on how big you want the bead to be. For tube beads, cut the log into equal lengths and pierce the center with a toothpick or knitting needle. Pierce the bead from both ends to get neat holes; if you just push the stick straight through, make sure that you smooth the rough edges where the stick emerges.

Round beads are made in the same way but each piece of clay is shaped into a ball in the palms of your hands. Pierce holes with a toothpick as above. Square beads are also made from a long log that is then flattened into a square against the edge of a knife or piece of wood. Cut to size and pierce as before. Add texture and detail to plain beads of any shape by pressing modeling tools, coins, and so on, against the surface, or by adding small strips or dots of other colors.

Experiment with several colors, for more exciting finishes, such as marbling or millefiori. To create a marbled effect, roll out logs of two or more colors and wrap them around each other. Knead these together, roll them back into a larger log, folding it in half and twisting until the colors are blended. Be careful not to knead too much or the individual colors will disappear and the clay will eventually return to a new, single color. Shape beads as described above.

Millefiori or "thousand flower" beads are slightly more complicated, but rewarding to make once you have mastered the techniques. Begin with a core color—either a plain log or two colors rolled together. Then place other logs in different colors around the core, completely surrounding it. The colors are usually placed in a regular pattern and must be gently pressed together to ensure no air is trapped inside. The whole cane is then wrapped in another sheet of clay, carefully rolled out to a diameter of about ¼ inch / .5 cm, and cut into tiny slices that are pressed on an unbaked base bead to cover it.

Safety Note

Always read the instructions given on the polymer clay package. This clay gives off fumes, especially as it bakes, and should be used in a well-ventilated room.

Fabric Beads

Using paper is one of the easiest and cheapest ways to make beads. The simplest papier-mâché beads can be made by shaping pieces of newspaper into a ball and then layering pasted strips of newspaper over it. For a smoother finish, layer the paper strips over a ball of plasticine. When the ball is completely dry, cut it in half with a craft knife and remove the plasticine to lighten the paper beads. Glue the two halves of the bead back together and conceal the joint with another layer of paper before decorating.

To make rolled paper beads, use old wrapping paper or magazines, or paint your own designs onto plain paper; then cut into strips or elongated triangles, and roll up tightly around a toothpick. To give the finished beads a sheen and a durable finish, paint them with clear nail polish.

Paper Beads

You can use fabric to make all kinds of beads that can be decorated with embroidery or sewn stitches, or even with tiny beads. To make little puffs of fabric, cut the fabric out in circles, hem the edges, and draw up the edges. For tube beads, strips of fabric can be joined and gathered at either end. To give them shape, wrap them over a cardboard base or stuff with a little padding.

Wooden Beads & Pressed Cotton Beads

Most craft suppliers stock unvarnished wooden beads and pressed cotton balls in a variety of sizes. These are both easy to paint and decorate in your own individual style. Support the beads on wooden skewers, tops of pencils, or old paintbrush handles while painting, and leave to dry on a knitting needle stuck in a block of plasticine or polystyrene. Keep patterns simple. If you want to use several colors, let each color dry before starting the next. When you are finished, protect the surface with a coat of clear varnish or nail polish.

Miscellaneous Bead Ideas

Roll ordinary kitchen foil or colored candy foil wrappers to make bead shapes. Pierce the center with a sharp needle and thread into necklaces. Or add colored foil as a decorative final layer on a papier-mâché bead. Salt dough, which needs to bake in a low-temperature oven for several hours, is another good medium for making beads of different shapes. Both foil and clay can be painted and decorated to suit your design.

Pasta, seeds, nuts, and even washers can be painted, decorated, and strung into spectacular jewelry—no one will ever guess their origins. Use your imagination, and you will discover that all sorts of bits and pieces—safety pins, colorful paper clips, and even rubber bands can be turned into jewelry.

CREATING A DESIGN

Finding Inspiration

THE STARTING POINT IN ANY DESIGN IS FINDING INSPIRATION.

IDEAS FOR jewelry designs can come from a visit to a museum or a library. Look to the ancient Egyptian, Roman, and Celtic civilizations, as well as the more recent Arts and Crafts and Art Deco periods, for ideas. A walk in the country or along the seashore can put you in touch with one of the greatest and most economical design source libraries: Mother Nature. Flowers and foliage, rocks and minerals, insect and animal life all can spur the imagination. The sky provides us with the sun, moon, and star motifs that are perfect for interpreting into jewelry forms.

Don't forget the materials you have on hand. Beads and fabrics can fall accidentally and often haphazardly together to create striking and unusual combinations. Paints and decorative finishes are fun to experiment with. Clays can be molded into unusual shapes and given textured finishes.

Working Out a Design

Once you have found your inspiration, try to sketch out different ideas on paper. You will need a sketch book, tracing paper, pencils, colored crayons, felt tip markers (including gold and silver markers), an eraser, and a pencil sharpener. You don't have to draw works of art; rough sketches will suffice. Consider buying a special tray that has channels for the beads to easily plan and make necklaces and bracelets in two or three different lengths.

For simple designs, start with a center point of interest, such as one of the beads you intend to use. Decide on the length you want, then sketch the sides, keeping them symmetrical.

As a general rule, most necklaces and bracelets should be made from an uneven number of beads so that one will fall at the center. If you are adding a pendant or tassel decoration, however, use an even number of beads so that the pendant becomes the center point. To get the best visual balance with beads of different sizes, place the larger ones near the center and the smaller ones tapering off toward each end. The same principle also applies to any charms.

After working out your basic design, pick the thread, clasp, and end fittings. To calculate how many beads you will need, count how many beads fit into 1 inch / 2.5 cm, then multiply this by the length required. Write down the findings you will need next to your design sketch. If you want to try any unusual paint effects or create complex millefiori beads, experiment with paints on paper before moving on to a sample bead.

Long NECKLACES

Long necklaces are both beautiful and versatile. You can arrange them in double or triple strands, or simply let them hang long. Papier-mâché beads give the necklace texture and help keep long necklaces lightweight. Use polymer clays to create colorful beads that mimic real marble or Venetian glass (but are much less heavy), or to mold charms into stylized contemporary flower shapes. To create glamorous, retro designs, knot the strand midway for a 1920s flapper look. Or mix crystal and pearls to wear on a sparkling night out on the town.

Feel free to adapt the necklace designs that follow to suit your materials and needs. Try using jet black beads instead of pearls in the diamonds and pearls tassel necklace. Experiment with gold and colored stones for the Flowering Vine necklace. Use clays in strong jewel tones to transform the marbled beads into faux precious stones like lapis or malachite.

This technique can be used to make a variety of charm shapes. Consult books on the history of jewelry or take a trip to a museum for inspiration.

Consider how the charms will link together when you plan your design.

Use scraps of clay to practice shaping your designs and bake to check how it will work. (If the clay is rolled out too finely, it will become weak and brittle.)

To wire the charms like beads, use a head or eye pin to make a hole, and leave in when baking to harden.

Choose a neutral-colored clay if you plan to use a painted finish.

For a jazzier look, make charms in lots of different colors.

SYNTHETIC POLYMER CLAYS ARE ONE OF THE MOST versatile of the newer modeling materials available for jewelry-making, and can, with a little creativity, be fashioned into expensive-looking designs. The soft and pliable clay makes it easy to mold or sculpt into almost any kind of shape you can think of, from basic beads to more intricate designs like these contemporary, stylized flowers. When hardened in a low-temperature oven and varnished or painted, the finished pieces can imitate precious metals or the finest porcelain but have the advantage of not shattering into little pieces if dropped. The clays are available in a wonderful range of colors that you can use as they are, or blend with other colors. The finished pieces also take on a totally different look when decorated with glittering jewel stones and metallic paint.

Metallic paint, chain, and Fimo

FLOWERING VINE

Getting Started

Break off a piece of Fimo and knead with your thumbs and fingers until soft and pliable. To join the flower charms to the chain, use jump rings large enough to fit over a petal of the flower, with room to move. Fimo varnish and silver powder mixed together can be applied to the flowers as an alternative to metallic paint.

You Will Need

1.

Roll out the Fimo after kneading into a very fine sausage shape.

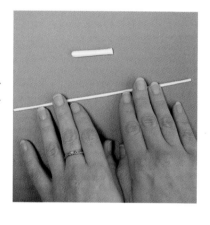

2.

Make a small loop at one end.

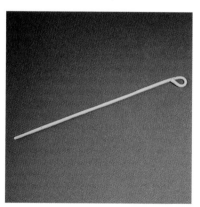

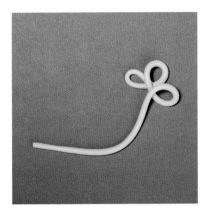

3.

Lift up the other end of the sausage and make another loop at a 45° angle to the first, working counterclockwise, then make another loop in the same way so that it is a mirror image of the first.

4.

Make the last loop to complete the shape and bring the Fimo to the center.

5.

Cut off any excess at the center point and then very gently flatten the flower slightly with your palm.

6.

Harden in a low-temperature oven following instructions for the Fimo. When cold, paint all the surfaces carefully with metallic paint. When dry, paint with varnish and leave for 24 hours before making into a necklace.

7. Use pliers to break the chain into even lengths. Count how many links are required for each piece and snap open the link one beyond this.

8. Use pliers to open a jump ring, slip the ring over the charm, and through the end link in the length of chain. Close securely. Repeat on the other side of the charm.

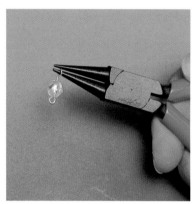

9. Insert an eye pin through a crystal bead. Trim excess wire with cutters, leaving enough wire to turn a loop with pliers on the opposite end to the eye.

10. Open up a jump ring, slip it through the free end of a length of chain, and through the loop on the crystal bead and close. Join the remaining loop on the bead to another length of chain in the same way. Join the last 2 charms to a necklace clasp instead of to the crystal bead.

11.

Glue jewel stones to the center of each flower to finish.

Variations on a Theme

Hearts are another variation on the basic theme. To add a glamorous sparkle, they have been linked by a chain to larger crystals taken from a chandelier (right).

In this contemporary design, Fimo is rolled into tube beads and a large "nugget" to make a pendant drop. Paint the shapes gold or silver and link together with a matching chain (far right).

Use vintage beads to produce an antique finish, especially for designs inspired by the past.

To make a larger tassel with more beaded strands, work each side of the necklace on three or four threads instead of two. Remember that tassels always look better with an odd number of strands.

Experiment by adding more beads to each single strand of thread. If you opt for more than two threads on each side, try beading all of them before bringing them back together through a single bead.

Twisting or braiding the divided strands can create spectacular effects.

Use the same basic techniques to create different effects with alternative bead styles. Try substituting bugle beads for the pearls, and glass rocailles for the crystals to give the necklace a more delicate finish.

THE DECADES OF THE 1920S AND 1930S, THE ERA of the flapper and of art deco design, produced truly creative jewelry design that is still very popular today. Style books on this period can be excellent sources of inspiration for your own individual designs. This 1930s-inspired necklace is worked in a sophisticated combination of pearls and rosettes of crystal beads, and finished with a central, elegant, beaded tassel that was all the rage at the time. The touch of sparkle from the light-reflecting crystals gives this particular bead combination the magic and formality perfect for evening wear. To transform this necklace for a more relaxed look, choose different colors, styles, and even bead sizes—try all wooden beads in contrasting colors, as in the wooden necklace in *Variations on a Theme*.

Scissors, cotton thread, and fine needles

DIAMONDS & PEARLS

Getting Started

Each side of this necklace comprises 2 pieces of thread, 44 inches / 112 cm long. The thread pair is divided, beaded individually, and then brought back together again to create the crystal rosettes. When each side is the length you want, take the threads of both through a large central bead and then bead each individual thread to form the tassel. Use an odd number of beaded strands for the tassels.

1. Cut 4 strands of thread to the length required for each side of the necklace (including the tassel) plus 12 inches / 31 cm. Knot the strands together in pairs and thread each pair through a calotte. With the knot sitting neatly in the cup of the calotte, use a pair of pliers to secure it firmly over the threads.

2. Working one side at a time, thread each length of cotton thread through a needle and then take both needles through 5 pearls and 1 crystal. Separate the threads and add 2 crystals to each. Bring the threads together again by taking both needles through a crystal. Pull the threads taut and push the beads back toward the calotte, making sure the crystals form an even shape.

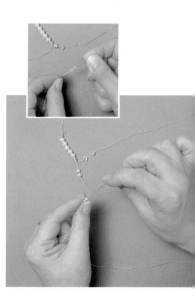

3. Repeat steps 2 and 3 until each side is the right length to begin working the tassel, making sure both sides are identical. Take all four strands through the diamanté rondelle and then through the large crystal bead.

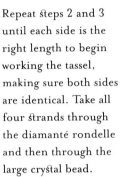

4. Work 2 of the 4 threads together. Thread each with alternating pearl and crystal beads to the length required. Wrap the thread around the last bead, and take the needle back through the rest of the beads on the strand and the large crystal.

5. When all the strands have been worked, knot the threads securely together between the crystal and the rondelle. Add a dab of glue to secure the knot if required. To finish, slip the loop of each calotte through a loop on the necklace clasp and secure using pliers.

Variations on a Theme

Wooden beads in contrasting colors give this necklace, which is worked on the entire length of 2 strands of thread, a more playful, less formal look than the diamonds and pearls project (right).

To complete the shimmering effect of this 3 strand necklace, a decorative filigree bell cap and hanger are added (far right).

37

Medium NECKLACES

Medium-length necklaces are easy for most people to wear and are perfect for adding just the right finishing touch to an outfit. You can make simple strings from a combination of interesting beads or, with a little inspiration, create more extravagant and unusual designs. Transform wrapping paper or handmade paper into glossy beads in minutes. Create festive necklaces from multicolored wooden beads cleverly linked by a simple length of chain. For a more international look, string a selection of antiqued silver charms in interesting shapes. Display a collection of beautiful shells for everyone to see by wearing them on a necklace interspersed with complementary beads. Combine fabric remnants with matching frosted beads to make a soft, pretty fabric puff necklace. To create a classic beaded necklace, use Fimo to make imitation millefiori, Venetian beads that offer a swirl of colors.

Create your own variations once you have mastered the techniques shown in the step-by-step projects. Make different style millefiori canes and use them to completely cover the base bead. Experiment with different color combinations and bead sizes to alter the look of the bold chain necklace. Bring in other objects from the seashore, like starfish, bits of glass, or driftwood, to give the shell necklace a truly natural look.

Handpainted Paper
BEADS

Design Tips

Spray or paint beads with a couple of coats of varnish to give them a more durable finish.

For totally unique beads, paint large sheets of paper with your own designs, experimenting with different paint effects, such as marbling, sponging, striping, and stippling.

To add a decorative touch, run a metallic pen along the edge of each paper strip before rolling up.

If you make your own paper, add interesting texture to the paper with the ends of colored thread, fabric bits, herbs, flowers, and grasses.

Recycle wrapping paper and colorful magazine pages for beads that cost next to nothing—if you don't like the finished effect, you can always paint them with acrylic paints or even nail polish.

YOU MIGHT REMEMBER TEARING STRIPS FROM magazines or catalogues to make paper bead necklaces when you were a child. Now you can make more sophisticated paper beads that even resemble pretty ceramic beads by choosing the right paper and using the right techniques. The skills to make these beads are easy to master, and once you've had a little practice you can have a wonderful time creating lots of different effects. Experiment with unusual papers as well as with traditional wrapping papers. Shiny foil designs, textured handmade papers, and even your own hand-painted plain paper can all be used to great effect. You can vary the shape of each bead by cutting paper strips to different lengths, widths, and shapes—the longer the strip, the fatter the bead, and the wider the strip, the longer the bead.

Varnish, spacer beads, calotte crimps, jump rings, clasp, and nylon thread

41

HANDPAINTED PAPER BEADS

Getting Started

These beads are made from painted paper cut into 2 different shapes, and then rolled and glued. Use 2 sheets of paper, about 16 x 18 inches / 41 x 46 cm in size. Cut nylon thread for the necklace into a length of 24 inches / 61 cm, with a little extra for knotting.

You Will Need

1.

Lay the sheet of paper out on a flat surface and paint on a stripe design. Leave to dry. Paint another sheet of paper in one of the colors used in the stripe design and use the tip of the brush to add texture. Leave to dry.

2.

Lay the striped paper face down with the stripes falling vertically. Mark one edge of the paper in 1-inch / 2.5 cm-intervals. On the opposite edge, mark ½ inch / 1 cm in, then mark 1-inch- / 2.5 cm-intervals. Connect the marks on opposite edges of the paper, forming long triangles. Lay the plain painted paper wrong side down on a flat surface and mark on the vertical edge intervals of ½ inch / 1 cm. Use a ruler to join the marks together in parallel lines.

FOR THE PAPER BEADS

2 large sheets of paper
Poster paints in several colors
Large paintbrush
Pencil
Long ruler
Scissors
Toothpick or wooden skewer
PVA glue
Spray or paint-on varnish

FOR THE NECKLACE

Needle
Nylon thread
2 calotte crimps
Gold spacer beads
1 head pin
3 jump rings
Necklace clasp
Pliers

3.

Cut out the strips you need. Discard outside edge strips. Roll triangles around a toothpick, starting at the widest end. Keep the roll tight with the tapering edges in the center. Roll the straight strips around a toothpick to form cylinder-shaped beads.

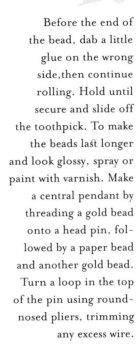

5.

Make a large knot in one end of the thread and place inside a calotte crimp. Close the calotte using pliers. String the paper beads onto the thread, alternating with gold spacer beads. Add the pendant when you reach the center front point, and work the second side of the necklace to match the first. Add a clasp and jump ring to the loops on the calotte crimps at the ends.

4.

Before the end of the bead, dab a little glue on the wrong side, then continue rolling. Hold until secure and slide off the toothpick. To make the beads last longer and look glossy, spray or paint with varnish. Make a central pendant by threading a gold bead onto a head pin, followed by a paper bead and another gold bead. Turn a loop in the top of the pin using round-nosed pliers, trimming any excess wire.

Variations on a Theme

Mix colorful wrapping paper beads with beads of a similar shape and coordinating color, and string into a necklace in any length you want (right).

Handmade papers that you can buy from arts and crafts shops or that you make yourself give the rolled beads an interesting texture (far right).

43

Practice making perfect loops in the top of a head pin using round-nosed pliers. It is important that the loops close securely over the chain links or the beads will fall off when worn.

If the holes of the bead are too big and the eye pins slip through the holes, add a small rocaille to act as a stopper bead.

When working with lots of colors or a mix of completely different beads, it is still important to balance the necklace. Too many large beads or beads of the same color on one side will spoil the effect. Working the necklace from the center will help you get the balance right.

Reuse beads from any broken necklaces you have, and look for interesting beads at flea markets, antique markets, or rummage sales.

THIS UNUSUAL NECKLACE IS MADE BY WIRING LOTS of colorful wooden beads onto a chain with gold eye pins to create a bold, festive design that completely covers the chain. The beads are relatively inexpensive and therefore affordable in the abundant quantities needed to make the necklace striking. You can also use plastic or glass beads, or even make your own out of papier-mâché or Fimo. For a really eclectic mix of beads, collect and string the odd beads you have in your bead box. For more restrained designs, work with a single color, two-tone colors, or a selection of hues, such as pretty pastels on a silver chain. Mixing together different-sized beads creates yet another look. Once you become skilled at wiring and linking the bead drops to the chain, you'll discover there are endless possibilities.

*Multicolor beads,
eye pins, jump rings,
and necklace clasp*

45

MARDI GRAS BAUBLES

Getting Started

Cut a length of chain to about 24 inches / 61 cm. To determine how many beads you need, decide whether you join the beads to every link or to every other link, then count up the number of links that you will use. (Ignore the first link at both ends—these will join to a clasp.) Then choose the same number of eye pins.

1.

Thread all but 4 beads onto an eye pin. Add a small stopper bead if the pin slips straight through the hole. Trim the wire to leave approximately ¼ inch / .5 cm for the loop.

2.

Use the tips of a pair of round-nosed pliers to turn the wire into a neat loop. Thread each of the remaining 4 beads onto an eye pin.

3.

Trim with wire cutters leaving about ½ inch / 1 cm. Use pliers to make a loop and then work the wire into a spiral.

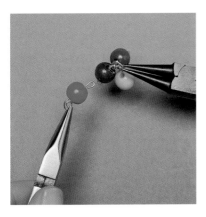

4. Open up a jump ring and thread through the eyes of the pins on the beads with spirals. Close the jump ring securely.

5. Open up a second jump ring and slip it through the first and the center front link on the chain. Close securely.

7. Join a jump ring to one end of the chain and a necklace clasp and jump ring to the other.

6. Open up the loops on the remaining beads and close again over a link in the chain, spacing them as needed.

Variations on a Theme

Gold eye pins join ruby and clear crystals to a chain to create this stunning necklace (right).

These papier-mâché animal charms (far right) were shaped from plasticine before being covered with pasted strips of paper, like the beads in *Pretty Papier-Mâché*.

Antiqued
CHARMS

Before starting, sketch out your ideas on paper or lay the beads out on a flat surface to plan the design.

Practice making perfect loops in the top of a head pin using round-nosed pliers. It is important that the loops close securely or the charms will fall off when the necklace is worn.

If the holes of the charm are so big that the eye pins slip through them, add a small matching bead or rocaille to act as a stopper bead.

Work the necklace backward from the center to help with getting the balance right.

Always select an odd number of charms—one for the center and an even number for either side of the necklace.

THIS STYLISH NECKLACE IS MADE FROM A selection of small silvery beads with a matte, almost antique finish that conjures up an international look. The decorative metal charms are hollow, so they are lightweight, and can be easily obtained from your bead supplier. As an alternative, you can use genuine silver charms that look a little tarnished. Or try shiny, highly polished, silvery beads to produce more of a refined effect. If you have collected them, use bits and pieces from broken earrings and neck-laces in a similar color. Whatever charms you decide to wire, just make sure that they are similar in size. You won't need to make this necklace symmetrical (that is, position the same beads in the same place on both sides of the necklace)—just check that the overall design is visually balanced.

Silvery beads, head pins, jump rings, necklace clasp, and crimp beads

ANTIQUED CHARMS

Getting Started

For this design, it isn't important to use exactly the same kind and number of beads on each side of the necklace. Just thread on similar-sized beads, and place the charms at regular intervals, checking that the overall effect is balanced. Use tiger tail or nylon line that is approximately 24 inches / 61 cm long.

You Will Need

Tiger tail or nylon line
2 crimp beads
Small silvery beads
11 to 15 hollow metal beads
Same number of head pins
Wire cutters
Round-nosed pliers
Needle-nosed pliers
11 to 15 jump rings
Small split ring
Necklace clasp

1.

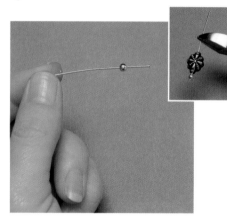

Thread a small metal bead onto a head pin. Add a metal charm and trim the wire leaving approximately ⅜ inch / 1 cm.

2.

Use round-nosed pliers to turn a loop in the top of the wire.

3.

Cut the tiger tail to the required length. Thread on a crimp bead and push it close to one end. Make a loop and push the end of the tiger tail back through the crimp bead. Squeeze the crimp beads tightly with needle-nosed pliers to secure the loop.

4. Thread on beads, positioning them in matching pairs wherever you want to place a charm.

5. Slip a jump ring through the top of each charm and loop it over the tiger tail, between a pair of beads. Close to secure.

6. Thread on a crimp bead, make a loop in the tiger tail, and take the end back through the crimp. Squeeze tightly with pliers. Join a necklace clasp to the loop.

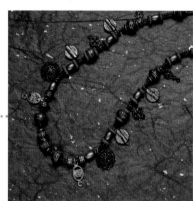

Variations on a Theme

For a necklace that makes a bolder statement, use larger charms, like these gold and amber washers, spirals, and filigree shapes (right).

Slightly tarnished silver charms give this necklace a brilliant black onyx look (far right).

Magnificent
MILLEFIORI

A book on the history of beads or even old pieces of jewelry can provide inspiration for millefiori designs.

Sketch designs on paper and color with felt-tip pens or paints that match the colors of the clays.

Cut out wedges of clay and substitute for or alternate with logs to get another style of design.

Experiment with base beads in different shapes—tubes, squares, cylinders, and ovals are all easy to mold in your hands.

Heavy clay beads need to be strung on a strong thread like nylon, but if you prefer to use a cotton or silk in a matching color use 4 to 6 strands together and knot the thread between each bead.

Use beads in brilliant contrasting colors or simple combinations like black and white.

MILLEFIORI BEADS WERE ORIGINALLY MADE FROM glass by the Venetians and were highly sought after all over the world. Translated, "Millefiori" means "a thousand flowers" because the Venetians could get so many slices of the same flower from one glass cane. Today, the same basic techniques can be applied to polymer clays to create spectacular beads like the ones shown here. Different colored clays in striking combinations are rolled and wrapped around each other to make the "millefiori cane." This is carefully and gently rolled to form a much narrower cane from which fine slices are cut and used to cover a plain base bead. The technique is not as difficult to master as it may seem and the cane can be used to make amazing jewelry on its own.

Fimo and scissors

MAGNIFICENT MILLEFIORI

Getting Started

Decorations for these beads are sliced from a tube or "cane"
made of 7 logs of clay wrapped together. Knead the Fimo with your
thumbs and fingers until really soft and pliable, to prevent cracks and to
make it much easier to roll. Wash your hands when changing colors to
prevent one hue rubbing off on another. Cut the nylon thread
to a length of 24 inches / 61 cm plus 6 inches / 15 cm for knotting.

You Will Need

FOR THE MILLEFIORI CANE

Fimo in 4 different colors
Rolling pin
Craft knife

FOR THE BASE BEADS

Fimo in other colors to go with the cane
Wooden skewer
Varnish

FOR THE NECKLACE

Nylon thread
2 calotte crimps
Sewing needle
Small spacer beads
Necklace clasp
Pliers

2.

From a block of Fimo in a contrasting color, roll out a sheet ⅛ inch / 3 mm thick and large enough to wrap over the log. Smooth the seam and then gently compress and roll the wrapped log between the palms of your hands.

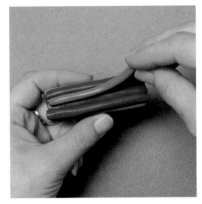

1.

To make the center of the cane, use the palms of your hands to roll out a log from 1 color of Fimo approximately ¼ inch / 6 mm in diameter.

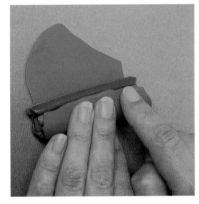

4.

Roll out another sheet of Fimo in one of the colors used for the center and wrap around the cane. Smooth the seam and gently compress together. You may find it easier to cut the cane into shorter lengths before wrapping with the last sheet of Fimo.

3.

Roll out 3 logs of equal diameter from each of the remaining colors, and build the cane by alternating the logs around the center, as shown. Gently compress together and roll between the palms of your hands.

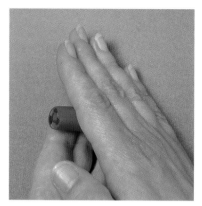

5. Roll the cane carefully and evenly between the palms of your hands first, then on a flat surface until the diameter is about ¼ inch / 6 mm.

6. To make base beads, roll them into balls or tubes. Cut off the misshapen end of the cane, then cut the rest into thin slices. Cover each bead with millefiori slices and roll gently in your palms to merge them together.

7. Leave the beads for several hours. Pierce a central hole in each using a wooden skewer or knitting needle. Bake in a low temperature oven, following instructions. Apply a coat of varnish to bring out all the colors. Let dry for 24 hours before threading the beads.

Completing the Necklace

Cut the nylon thread to the length required, make a large knot in one end, and take the other end through a calotte. With the knot sitting neatly in the cup of the calotte, use pliers to secure the thread. String the beads on in the order you want, placing small spacer beads between each clay bead. Knot the remaining end of thread close to the last bead and secure to a calotte. Attach necklace clasp to loops on each calotte, closing the loops with pliers to secure.

Variations on a Theme

Using 3 simple colors can also be very effective (right).

Make up a geometric design, like colorful squares, as a variation on the traditional flower-influenced canes (far right).

57

Choker
NECKLACES

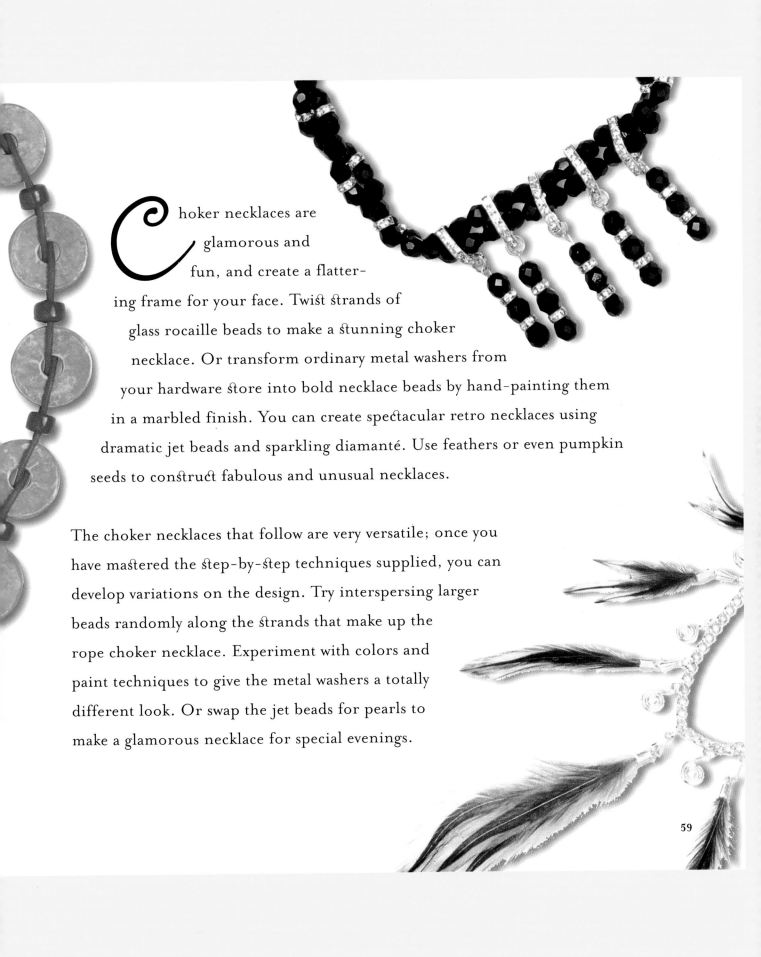

Choker necklaces are glamorous and fun, and create a flattering frame for your face. Twist strands of glass rocaille beads to make a stunning choker necklace. Or transform ordinary metal washers from your hardware store into bold necklace beads by hand-painting them in a marbled finish. You can create spectacular retro necklaces using dramatic jet beads and sparkling diamanté. Use feathers or even pumpkin seeds to construct fabulous and unusual necklaces.

The choker necklaces that follow are very versatile; once you have mastered the step-by-step techniques supplied, you can develop variations on the design. Try interspersing larger beads randomly along the strands that make up the rope choker necklace. Experiment with colors and paint techniques to give the metal washers a totally different look. Or swap the jet beads for pearls to make a glamorous necklace for special evenings.

Shimmering MOONSTONES

It is essential to work in good light when stringing very small beads.

Delicate beads look best strung on a strong silk thread or invisible thread—anything heavier will spoil the effect.

Add the occasional large bead to a strand to give the necklace a different scale.

The more bead strands used to make up the choker, the more luxurious the finished look.

Instead of twisting the strands around each other, make them long enough to tie into a central knot.

For a central focus point, make a coordinating bead from Fimo or papier-mâché with a hole large enough to take all of the strands.

Look for and use unusual necklace clasps or recycled ones from broken necklaces.

TINY GLASS ROCAILLE BEADS ARE OFTEN USED in bead embroidery with bugle beads and sequins, but they also look fabulous strung into necklaces in a wide range of colors or worked in subtle color combinations to match a favorite outfit. For this rope choker, the beads are threaded onto fine silk threads that are then twisted around each other to create the rope style. Threading on all the beads for each strand takes a little patience but the finished design is worth the effort. The more strands you make, the more lavish the necklace will look. Twisting the strands together to form a "rope" is a classic jewelry design often worked in pearls, but there are many variations on this style. Experiment by twisting the strands in groups and then all together, and try loosely braiding groups of strands for another look.

Rocaille beads and scissors

61

SHIMMERING MOONSTONES

Getting Started

This necklace is made up of 4 groups of bead strands, with 3 bead strands in each group. Work 2 of these groups in the same color, and the other 2 in different, coordinating colors. Use a beading needle to thread several of the smaller beads onto the needle at once. Cut the thread into choker length, about 12 inches / 31 cm without the clasp, plus 1 inch / 2.5 cm to allow for twisting and another 12 inches / 31 cm for easy threading and knotting.

You Will Need

Tiny glass beads in 3 different colors
Strong silk or invisible thread
Beading needle
8 calotte crimps
Pliers
4 jump rings
2 head pins
2 bell caps
Wire cutters
Necklace clasp

1.

Tie one end of a strand to a large stopper bead to prevent beads falling off while you work and thread on beads to the desired length. Tie the free end of the thread to a stopper bead and work another 2 strands to make up the group.

2.

Untie stopper beads and knot the 3 threads together. Slip the knot into a side-opening calotte, using pliers to close and secure the thread. At the other end, knot the threads together close to the last beads and secure with a calotte. Repeat for all strands.

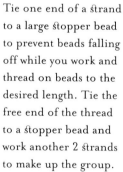

Using pliers, open up a tiny jump ring, slip it through the loops of all the calottes at one end, and close to secure. Repeat for the opposite end.

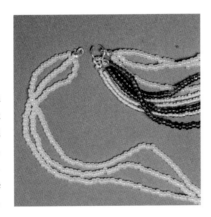

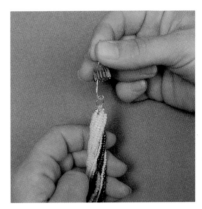

Use pliers to turn a loop at one end of a head pin, slipping it through the jump ring before closing securely. Push the free end of the head pin through a bell cap hole. Pull it as far as it will go so that calottes and jump ring are covered. Trim the wire and turn another loop.

Open up a jump ring and insert through the loop on the bell cap and through the loop on one part of the necklace clasp. Close securely using pliers.

Variations on a Theme

Larger glass beads have been used to make this stunning black and white necklace (right) and the five-hole filigree hanger adds a decorative finishing touch.

To create a really special necklace, use lots of bead strands together and add larger beads randomly along a few of the strands (far right).

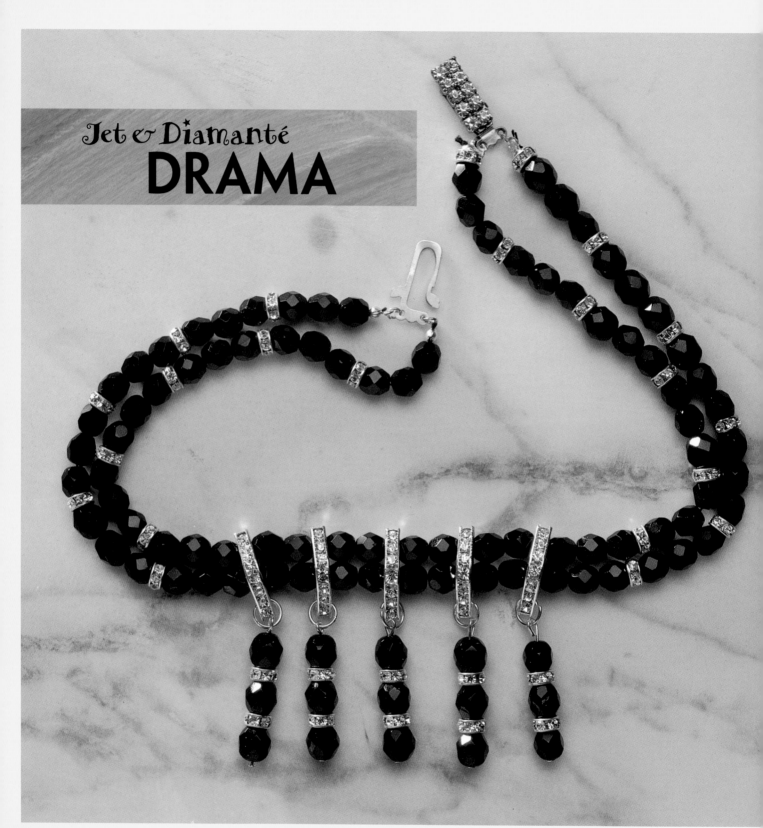

Jet & Diamanté
DRAMA

To avoid any pitfalls, work out more complex designs on paper before starting this necklace.

Measure your neck with a longer bead necklace or a string, following the curve of your neck.

Avoid making the necklace too short or it will look like it is strangling you.

Diamanté rondelles and spacers are quite expensive, so use them sparingly between groups of beads or substitute with tiny faceted crystal for a similar effect.

Scour antique markets, flea markets, and rummage sales for old clasps or necklaces that you can restring.

THE CLASSIC COMBINATION OF JET AND diamanté has existed in jewelry design for centuries. Real jet beads are expensive, but you can recreate the look with imitation replicas in glass or plastic. Faceted glass beads are the best choice; they are heavier and have a more realistic finish than their plastic equivalents. You can make a simple but striking necklace by just stringing the beads together with diamanté rondelles placed between each bead or bead group. More intricate designs, like the jet and diamanté necklace described here, have a greater impact especially when worked on several strands threaded through dramatic diamanté spacers. This design is also finished with an old clasp to give it the look of a genuine antique. Start a collection of unusual clasps to add a special finish to any of your designs.

Cotton thread, black, faceted beads, diamanté rondelles, and spacer bars

65

JET & DIAMANTÉ DRAMA

Getting Started

To make this 14 inch / 36 cm choker, cut black cotton thread into 4 strands of 20 inches / 51 cm each. Use the extra 6 inches / 15 cm for knotting and easy threading. The diamanté spacer bars have 3 holes: 2 holes for threading strands of double thread, and a third hole to join a jump ring and hanging beaded pin.

You Will Need

Strong black cotton thread
4 calotte crimps
Round-nosed pliers
Needle-nosed pliers
Sewing needle
Small black, faceted beads
& diamanté rondelles
5 3-hole diamanté spacer bars
5 head pins
5 jump rings
Necklace clasp with 2 holes

1.

Knot the threads together in pairs. Secure each knot within a calotte crimp.

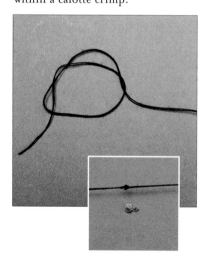

2.

Thread a pair through a needle and string on the beads in the pattern required. For this design the black beads were strung in groups of 3, followed by a diamanté rondelle.

3.

Work the bead pattern to the start of the center design and replace the rondelle with a spacer bar, taking the needle through the top hole.

4.

Add two beads and take the needle through the next spacer bar making sure it goes through the top hole again. Repeat until all the spacer bars are threaded on. Complete the string to match the first side. Use a needle to pull the knot close to the last bead.

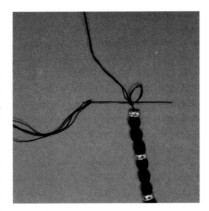

5.

Work the second thread pair in the same way.

6.

Thread alternating beads and diamanté rondelles onto a head pin and turn a loop at the top of the pin with round-nosed pliers. Open up a jump ring and push it through both the bottom loop of a spacer bar and the loop on the beaded pin. Close to secure and attach the loop on each calotte to the holes on the necklace clasp, opening and closing them with pliers.

Variations on a Theme

Larger beads and clear crystals (right) combine to create a more contemporary design. Smaller black beads interspersed with small crystals produce a classic and delicate look (far right).

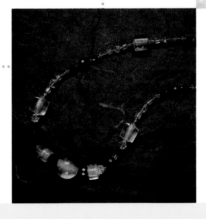

Silvery SEEDS

Spray painting is the easiest way to color tiny seeds but if you have the time and the patience you will get a superior finish if you hand paint each seed.

Some spray varnishes and spray paints do not work together, so test them on a handful of seeds before continuing to make the necklace.

Spray the seeds in batches of the same color and string onto the thread in alternating colors or in groups of the same colors.

Use a fine needle and thread. Anything thicker will split the seeds (unless they have several coats of varnish).

To create a uniform look, insert the needle in the same place on each seed. For a varied effect, try moving the needle position each time.

Add beads between each seed to make them go further or for a striking look, string them all together.

THE SUPERMARKET SHELF CAN BE A SURPRISINGLY inspirational place to look for materials to make jewelry. With just a little creativity you can convert simple pasta shapes, lentils, or even dried seeds from melons or pumpkins into delightful necklace charms. They can be strung together on invisible thread or glued to cardboard to make motifs to hang as charms or as a central pendant. Or attach them to special pendant findings sprinkled on a chain, as in the ingenious gourd seed and chain necklace (See *Variations on a Theme*). This delicate seed necklace with its silver teeth and pretty central pendant is made from pumpkin seeds bought from a health store. The seeds are varnished to give them a more durable finish and coated with a metallic paint to imitate the look of expensive precious metals. You can also use other paint colors to match the necklace to a favorite outfit.

Silver spray paint, invisible thread, and glass rocaille beads

SILVERY SEEDS

Getting Started

Pumpkin seeds are spray-painted and then glued to a cardboard circle to make the central pendant for this necklace. The remaining seeds are pierced with a fine needle and strung along a piece of invisible thread 20 inches / 51 cm long (choker length plus an extra 6 inches / 15 cm for knotting and easy threading).

You Will Need

Pumpkin seeds
Newspaper
Silver spray paint
Silver marker pen
Spray or paint-on varnish
Invisible thread
2 calotte crimps
Fine sewing needle
Small glass rocaille beads in several hues
Cardboard
Craft glue
Pendant finding
Necklace clasp
Jump rings
Pliers

1.

Scatter the seeds over a sheet of newspaper and spray the paint following instructions on the can—it is important to work in a well-ventilated area, preferably outside. Leave to dry and then turn the seeds over to spray the other side.

2.

Use a marker pen to touch up any areas the paint has missed, though the seeds also look attractive with some of the natural color showing through the paint.

3.

Cut out a small cardboard circle approximately ½ inch / 1 cm in diameter and paint it silver. Glue 4 seeds to the cardboard, forming a cross shape radiating from the center point. Leave to dry. Glue 4 more seeds to fill in the gaps as shown and leave to dry.

4.

Carefully pierce a hole at the top of 1 seed—not too close to the point or it will snap off—and open out the pendant finding, gently pushing the point through the holes as shown, squeezing it together between your fingers.

5.

Make a large knot in one end of the invisible thread and slip it into the "cup" of a calotte crimp. Press both sides of the crimp together using pliers. Thread the needle and work the necklace to the center point adding groups of rocailles between each seed. Pierce each seed in approximately the same position each time to get a uniform finished look.

6.

Slip a jump ring through the top loop of the pendant and thread onto the necklace. Work the second side of the necklace. Knot the thread close to the last group of rocailles and secure in a calotte crimp. Attach a necklace clasp to 1 calotte and jump ring to the other.

Variations on a Theme

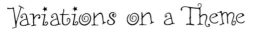

This striking necklace (right) has charms made from gourd seeds that were painted, varnished, and then fixed to pendant findings hung from a chain.

To create a totally different look, hang several striped sunflower seed charms from the necklace and intersperse them with black beads (far right).

71

Basic BRACELETS

Basic bracelets can be as bold or as discreet as you like depending on the style of the design and the materials you choose to use. You can make sassy cuffs from brightly painted cork slices strung onto elastic; transform a simple circle of cardboard into a striking contemporary bangle using basic papier-mâché techniques; or create beautiful effects with ordinary safety pins and a few beads.

When designing basic bracelets, consider the overall size and balance of the design. If you use your hands a lot, a bracelet will be irritating if it is too big and gets in the way. You should be able to get the bracelet on and off your wrist easily, so choose a clasp that is easy to open with one hand or thread the beads or bead substitutes onto fine elastic. Shirring elastic is ideal but it is a good idea to work with a double thread on designs that use heavy beads. Try decorative fancy cord elastic available in fun, bright colors or metallic finishes to color-coordinate with the beads. Be careful to balance your design, making sure that any central detail is perfectly positioned and any repeated motifs (like a group of beads) are spaced at regular intervals along the bracelet.

Once you have mastered the step-by-step techniques, you can play with each basic bracelet design to make an attractive variation on a theme. Paint cork slices with decorative details or simply sand and varnish them to reveal their true natural beauty. Experiment with safety pins and beads in different sizes. Swap the hematite and pearl beads for a stunning collection of ornate buttons to make a glamorous bracelet for special occasions.

Beaded
BRAIDS

DECORATIVE BRAIDS ARE USUALLY USED TO TRIM fashion items or furnishings for the home, but here they have been completely transformed into unusual bracelets. Braid, ribbons, and even fancy cords can all be jazzed up and given a new purpose with simple bead embroidery. For a subtle, sophisticated look, choose a design that highlights the pattern or shape of the braid; or to create really impressive bracelets, completely cover the ribbon or braid with a collection of different ornate beads, buttons, or a combination of both.

You Will Need

A length of braid
Beads
Tailor's chalk
Sewing needle
Sewing thread or
invisible thread
Seed beads

Getting Started

Use invisible thread or sewing thread that matches the beads and braid you are working with. The seed beads should be in colors that coordinate with the other materials as well.

BEADED BRAIDS

1.

Cut a length of braid long enough to fit around your wrist, plus enough for turnings. Oversew or glue raw ends to neaten.

2.

Lay the braid out on a flat surface and work out your design. Use tailor's chalk to mark the required position for each bead.

3.

Sew each bead in place individually, making sure it is secure.

4.

Join a double thread to the center of an end. String on 3 beads that match those used to work the design, then fasten off the thread close to the start position so that the beads form a "tab." At the opposite end, join a double thread to the center and thread on enough seed beads to make a loop that will slip neatly over the "tab" to join the two sides of the braid together.

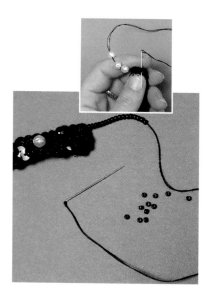

Variations on a Theme

1. Using invisible thread, sew coordinating beads to a velvet scalloped braid, attaching them between scallops.

2. Add a scalloped edge in contrasting silvery beads by threading 7 beads onto the thread before taking it through one of the larger beads.

3. Take the thread through another silvery bead and back through the large bead used in step 1. Continue until the length of the braid has been worked on both sides.

4. Oversew a clasp to one end and a jump ring to the other. Put a blob of super glue on the joint of the jump ring to prevent the thread from slipping through.

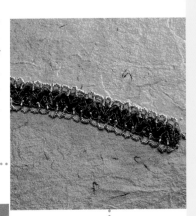

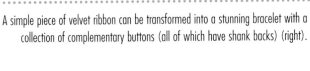

A simple piece of velvet ribbon can be transformed into a stunning bracelet with a collection of complementary buttons (all of which have shank backs) (right).

77

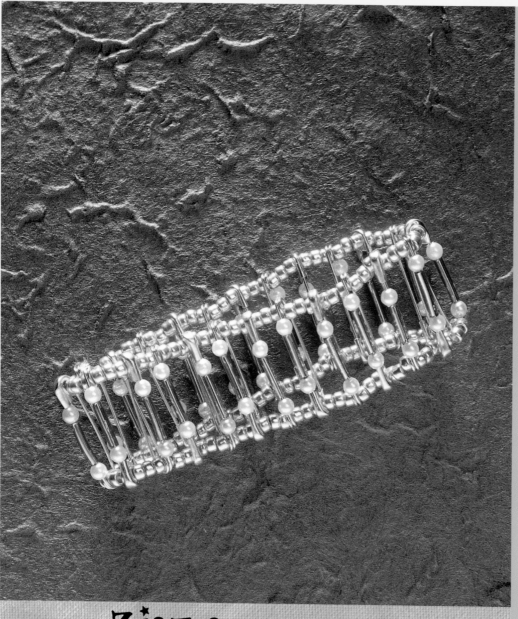

Zigzag GLITTER

Design Tips

Sketch your designs out first. Regular patterns make the most impressive results.

Smaller pins look best decorated with tiny rocailles or bugle beads.

Experiment with different-sized pins—larger ones can be transformed into quite bold designs and will take bigger beads.

To achieve the best shape, thread the pins onto the elastic alternately through the head and the tail.

Mixing gold- and silver-colored pins of the same size can create a stylish finish.

Use coordinating beads to separate the pins and make them go further if you only have a few.

Look for different colors of shirring elastic to coordinate with the bead design. Try gold or silver elastic to produce a more expensive-looking finished design.

THE ORDINARY SAFETY PIN HAS BECOME THE

height of fashion more than once—it was an essential part
of punk rock fashion popular in the late 1970s and
then again more recently, when is was featured holding together
very expensive designer dresses. Decorated with bugle beads and
tiny pearls in pretty color
combinations, safety pins can be
threaded together in myriad
patterns to make unique pieces
of jewelry.

You Will Need

Small safety pins
Bugle beads and small pearls
Pliers
Sewing needle
Shirring elastic
2 large beads
Gold rocailles
Glue

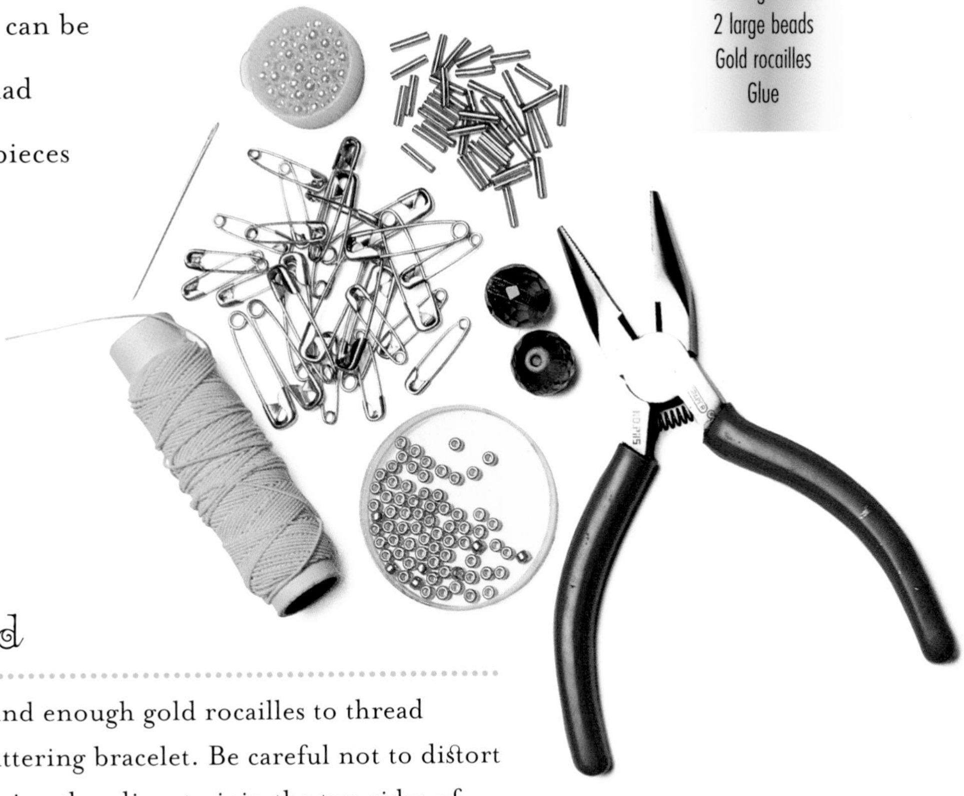

Getting Started

Select about 22 safety pins and enough gold rocailles to thread
between the pins for this glittering bracelet. Be careful not to distort
the shape of the pin when using the pliers to join the two sides of
the heads.

ZIGZAG GLITTER

1. Thread the beads onto each safety pin in the order required by your design.

2. The head of each pin is closed so the elastic will not slip out. Using a pair of pliers, gently bring both sides of the head together.

3. Using the pliers again, carefully squeeze together the edges of the head that hold the actual "pin."

4. Thread the needle with shirring elastic and secure a large bead to prevent the design from falling off as you work. Take the needle through the tail of a pin, then through the spacer beads and head of the next pin. Alternate the pins and add the same amount of beads between them until they fit around your wrist when the elastic is slightly stretched.

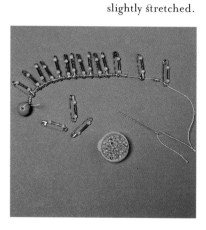

5.

Knot the elastic securely and add a blob of glue to strengthen it. To achieve a neater finish, push the knot inside a spacer bead to conceal it.

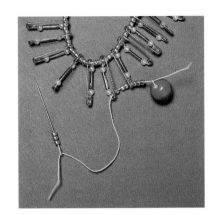

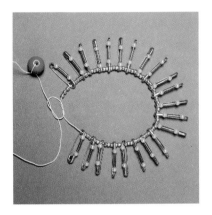

6.

Thread the elastic through the needle and tie it to a large bead again. Take the needle through the other end of the pins, adding the same number of beads between pins. Knot and finish in the same way as in step 5.

Variations on a Theme

Large silver pins look great threaded with long silver bugle beads and faux pearls. To create the stripe effect the pins with bugles have been threaded onto the elastic in pairs, with heads and tails facing and the pearl pins flipped in the opposite direction (right).

Plastic beads that look like amber have been used to make this cuff (far right).

81

Experiment with different types of fabric. Paint the PVA on a test piece of fabric first to check how many coats will be needed to get the rigidity you require.

PVA gives some fabrics an obvious shine. Do a test piece and check that you are happy with the finish.

You can achieve different effects by painting or embroidering the fabric first. Make sure you do a small test piece and paint with PVA as some embroidery threads can run colors.

Cut motifs in different shapes, such as hearts or daisies, to cover the fabric joint.

To make textured fabrics, such as linen, look expensively gilded, lightly brush them with metallic paint.

Fabric &
COPPER CUFF

THE USE OF FABRIC IN JEWELRY DESIGN IS BECOMING more and more popular. This "soft" jewelry offers endless opportunities for innovative ideas. Even traditional crafts such as embroidery, quilting, and patchwork can all be applied to different jewelry designs. Stiffening fabric with PVA glue gives it another dimension, as this bangle bracelet illustrates. It is made from a strip of inexpensive linen scrim that has been painted with PVA glue. The PVA gives the fabric a clear plastic coating, almost invisible to the eye, that helps keep it rigid and in shape. For a decorative finishing touch, spirals and a plain medallion motif have been glued to a diamond of fabric. These were made from a garden plant label, but you can also buy sheet copper from craft and sculpting suppliers. This kind of jewelry is pure fun but obviously is not as durable as anything made out of metal or plastic.

Getting Started

To determine the right size of fabric to use for this bracelet, cut a strip of fabric 2" / 5 cm wide. Fold to form a circle that will fit easily over your hand. Add a little extra fabric for the overlap. Make sure you use clear-drying glue that is suitable for metal surfaces.

You Will Need

Linen scrim cloth
Scissors
Needle
Matching thread
PVA glue
Paintbrush
Pin
Copper tag, plant label,
or small piece of sheet copper
Copper wire
Wire cutters
Pliers
All-purpose, clear-drying glue

FABRIC & COPPER CUFF

1.

Neaten any raw edges of the cloth by gluing them to the side of the cloth that will not be seen. Cut out 2, 2 inch / 5 cm squares for the central motif and glue them together.

2.

Make a tuck in each short end of fabric and secure it with a few oversew stitches.

3.

Pour the PVA into a dish and, resting the fabric on a ceramic surface, paint the side that will not show with PVA, making sure the glue goes into the folds formed by the tucks. Paint the center motif and leave it on a ceramic surface.

4.

Wrap the fabric bangle around a round plastic squeeze bottle or ceramic dish that has been rubbed with soft soap or Vaseline so that the fabric can be easily removed when dry. Pin it in place and let it dry.

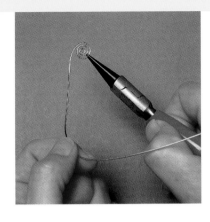

5. Cut the tie of the copper plant label in half. Turn each half around the tips of round-nosed pliers to make decorative spirals.

6. Cut a 1 inch / 2.5 cm square of copper from the plant label, and using a suitable adhesive, glue it to the center of a side of the motif.

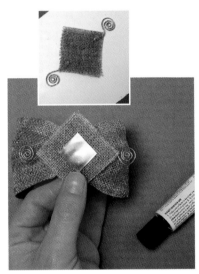

7. Turn the fabric motif on its side to make a diamond and glue the spirals to the wrong side as shown. Let dry. Glue the motif to the stiffened bangle, covering the joint.

Variations on a Theme

Using red and white gingham this time, the center is a neatened strip of fabric that has been stiffened and wrapped around tightly (right).

Narrow strips of candy-striped cotton have been painted with PVA and wrapped around an ordinary plastic bangle, giving it a brand new look (far right).

Charm
BRACELETS

You can make all kinds of charm bracelets, whether you use fun, simple beads, daring sequins, or even ordinary metal washers. Shells collected from the seashore can be drilled and wired to make charms that look wonderful falling from a raffia braid. Or mold, roll, and sculpt modeling clay into an eclectic mix of inspired shapes, from playing-card motifs to millefiori slices.

When hanging charms around a bracelet, it is especially important to work out your design. Consider the weight of the charms before choosing a basic bracelet of beads or a length of chain. Space charms evenly along the length of the bracelet for the best effect. It is also important to select a clasp that is easy to open with one hand so that getting the bracelet on and off is effortless. The balance of the design is also crucial; hang large charms from a medium or heavy chain, not a fine chain. In most cases it is better if the design is worked symmetrically, but when using a great number of the same beads, a mistake will hardly be noticeable.

The bracelets that follow are designed to fire your imagination and spur you on to create your own variations once you have mastered the techniques shown in the step-by-step projects. Design different styles of millefiori canes to slice and turn into colorful charms. Experiment with other ways of linking metal washers, and vary the color combinations and sizes of the bead charms to alter the look of the *Toolbox Pearls* bracelet. Bring in other elements of the sea to give the shell charm bracelet a truly natural look. Or research the myriad colors of mosaic tiles to get inspiration for your own variation on the tile charm bracelet.

87

Sparkling SEQUINS

SEQUINS DO NOT NORMALLY SPRING TO MIND WHEN considering materials for making bracelets, but they can be made into quite spectacular and unusual designs. They are available in a variety of shapes, a kaleidoscopic range of colors, and are inexpensive, all of which makes them perfect for fun jewelry designs. Sequin motifs in the shape of flowers, leaves, birds, and butterflies make fun charms suspended from a sequin or bead bracelet, while the classic smooth-surface discs look stylish, especially if they have a hologram finish. You can mix them together in wild color combinations or two-tone shades. Sequins that come with holes to one side are the easiest to use and can be made into instant charms, but other designs can be used too. They are all easy to pierce with the point of a needle.

You Will Need

Flower-shaped sequins
Rocaille beads
Clear-drying craft glue
Toothpick
Needle
Jump rings
Eye pins
Round-nosed pliers
Wire cutters
Nylon thread or tiger tail
2 calotte crimps
Gold rocaille beads
Clasp

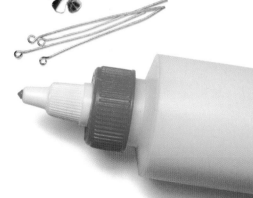

Getting Started

You will need lots of tiny rocaille beads that color-coordinate with the flower-shaped sequins, as well as gold rocaille beads. The number of sequin charms that you use will vary depending on how close together you attach them.

SPARKLING SEQUINS

1.

Glue rocaille beads in shades of the same color over the center hole of each flower sequin that will be used as a charm. The number of charms needed will vary depending on how close together you attach them.

2.

Use the point of a needle to make a small hole in a petal of each flower sequin to attach a jump ring. Twist the jump rings to open and insert them through the hole on each sequin that will be made into a charm.

3.

Thread 3 or 4 gold rocailles onto an eye pin. Trim the pin with wire cutters so that approximately ⅜ inch / 1 cm extends beyond the beads. Turn this into a loop using the tips of pliers.

4.

Measure and cut your chosen thread to fit around your wrist with room for knots, then knot the end and secure it to a calotte crimp. Thread on the sequins, taking the thread through the center hole with gold beads spaced between each sequin, adding charms as you work.

Variations on a Theme

5.

When the bracelet reaches the right length, finish it off with another knot secured in a calotte crimp. Twist open 2 jump rings and attach them to each calotte crimp. Complete the bracelet by attaching a clasp to a jump ring.

2.

Insert an open jump ring through each hole and then through the link on the chain at the same time. Close the jump ring securely.

1.

Hologram disc sequins can be made into fun bracelets. Cut a length of chain to fit your wrist and count the number of links on the chain. Choose a corresponding number of sequins, and use a needle to pierce a hole close to an edge of each sequin.

3.

The result is a melange of vividly colored hologram sequins, suspended from a length of chain.

Use just a few colors and fix interesting sequin shapes to make a more discreet elasticized bracelet (right).

91

Lay the tiles out in front of you and work out a color scheme, then select complementary beads to use as charms.

Experiment with different ways of linking the tiles together. Spirals worked from silver wire can be turned into figure-eight links, spring-like coils, and ornate spirals.

Try gluing material like crushed egg shells to papier-mâché tile shapes to give them texture as well as color.

You can get bags of irregularly shaped tiles in fabulous colors. These can be embedded in Polyfilla, plaster, or air-dry clay shapes to create the interesting patterns more frequently associated with the craft of mosaics. If they are loose after the base has dried, glue them in place.

Shimmering
MOSAICS

THESE MOSAIC TILES WERE DISCOVERED ON A STAND at a craft fair where the techniques for using them to create beautiful plaques and tabletops were being demonstrated. They illustrate perfectly how the most unusual materials can be transformed into stunning pieces of jewelry. The tiles are made from glass, which is not easy to drill, so large, thick jump rings are glued in place with epoxy adhesive so they can be linked together. The tiles can be obtained from craft specialists or tile suppliers. They come in a range of colors, from the pastels shown here to vivid pop art colors like orange, red, lime, green, and yellow.

You Will Need

6 small glass mosaic tiles
5 coordinating glass drop beads
12 large jump rings
Epoxy glue
7 small jump rings
5 triangle bails
Pliers
Two-part snap clasp

Getting Started

To keep the jump rings perfectly level as they dry, support them on another tile or lump of plasticine. Make sure that as you link the jump rings to the rings glued to the tiles, all the tiles are facing in the same direction.

SHIMMERINGS MOSAICS

1. Squeeze a small amount of the epoxy onto a piece of thick cardboard, carefully cleaning the tips of the tubes. Mix the glue together thoroughly. Be careful not to get any on yourself.

2. Close the large jump rings so they lie flat.

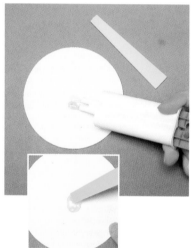

3. Following the guidelines given for the glue, stick a jump ring to the opposite corners on each tile. Make sure the ring extends beyond the tile so that you will be able to link tiles together later, when all rings are glued on.

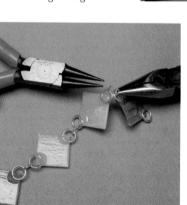

4. After the large jump rings have dried on each tile, twist open the smaller jump rings and slip them through a large jump ring on each of the tiles, making sure the tiles have their right sides facing the same direction.

5.

Close the jump rings
so they join exactly.

6.

Slip a triangle bail over
the small linking jump
ring and push one of its
ends into a side of the
hole at the top of a drop
bead. Line up the other
end of the bail with
the opposite hole in the
bead and squeeze
the ends together to
secure the bead.

7.

Twist open a small jump
ring and slip it through
the last large jump ring
at an end of the bracelet
and a part of the clasp.
Twist it back to secure.
Repeat for the other
part of the clasp to
complete the bracelet.

Variations on a Theme

The tiles themselves form the charms on this variation, with the jump rings glued
to just a corner. A copper chain from an old necklace was used for the bracelet (right).

For a completely different mosaic look, crushed eggshell has been applied
to a simple tile-shaped, papier-mâché base (far right).

1000 Flowers
CHARMS

Design Tips

A book on the history of beads or old pieces of jewelry can provide inspiration for different millefiori designs.

Sketch designs on paper and color with felt tip pens or paints that match the shades of the clays.

Use colors in brilliant contrasting combinations or simple pairs such as black and white.

Cut out wedges of clay and substitute for or alternate with logs to get another style of design.

Experiment with more graphic designs like stripes and squares to make a change from the traditional flower.

Use scraps of clay leftover from other projects to make multicolored canes.

The charms for this unusual bracelet are made from colorful synthetic clays, using a technique called *millefiori* which was developed by Venetian glass makers. The name means "a thousand flowers" because the Venetians could cut so many slices of the same flower pattern from one glass cane. The original glass beads were so highly prized all over the world that they were used as a form of currency to buy from the merchants who visited the busy port of Venice. The same basic techniques can be applied to polymer clays. The cane is built up around a core color that is surrounded by layers of different colors and finally wrapped in a sheet of clay. The completed cane is sliced to make the charms.

Getting Started

Knead the Fimo with your thumbs and fingers until really soft and pliable. This will make it much easier to roll and prevent cracks. Wash your hands when changing colors to prevent one from rubbing off on the other and spoiling the finished effect.

You Will Need

Blocks of Fimo in black, yellow, white, pink, and purple
Rolling pin
Craft knife
Toothpick
Varnish
15 to 20 triangle bails or large jump rings (1 for each charm)
Pliers
A length of chain (approximately 6" / 15.2 cm)
Clasp

1,000 FLOWERS CHARMS

For the core of the cane, roll out a log of yellow clay with a diameter of approximately ¼ inch / .6 cm. Roll out 4 logs in purple and 4 in white clay to a similar length and diameter.

Place the purple and white logs alternately around the yellow log, as shown. Gently compress them together and roll the resulting cane between the palms of your hands to press out any air bubbles. Make another cane in exactly the same way, and 2 more where you substitute pink for the purple, so you will have 4 canes in all. Roll out 5 logs in black, making them slightly larger in diameter than the previous logs. Lay 4 of these out on a flat surface and pinch them along one side to make them wedge-shaped. These will be used in the next step to fill in the gaps between the other logs to make the whole cane round.

Using the unpinched black log as the core, place the 4 canes you made in step 2 alternately around it, with black wedges filling the gaps in between the logs. Gently compress all the colors together so there are no air pockets.

Roll out a sheet from the black clay with a depth of approximately ⅛ inch / .3 cm.

5.

Wrap the sheet around the cane, smoothing the seam gently with your finger. Compress it together and roll it gently between your hands so there are no air pockets. You may find it easier to cut the cane into shorter lengths before wrapping with the last sheet of Fimo.

Completing the Bracelet

Count the number of links in the chain and decide whether to place the charms in every one or every other one. To join them to the chain, slip a triangle bail through a link in the chain and push one of its ends into one side of the hole at the top of a charm. Line up the other end of the bail with the opposite hole in the charm and squeeze the two ends together to secure the charm. Finish by attaching a clasp to one end of the chain and a jump ring to the other.

6.

With a craft knife, cut the cane into ¼ inch / .6 cm slices and reshape them with your hands. Pierce a hole in each slice close to the edge and bake them in a low-temperature oven following instructions on the Fimo package. A finishing coat of varnish will bring out all the colors; leave to dry for 24 hours before joining the slices to the chain.

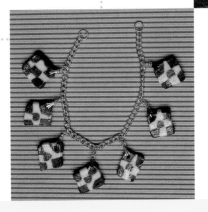

Variations on a Theme

To make these square charms (right), the clay is cut into small slabs that are then laid on top of one another to form the pattern.

Leftover clays from other projects have been used to make this striking design. The basic cane is the same for each charm but it was cut into smaller lengths and each wrapped with a different color (far right).

Multistrand & Linked
BRACELETS

M ultistrand and linked bracelets open up the possibility for more creative designs, using lots of different elements. You can create glamorous bracelets using faux pearls and diamanté and finish them with authentic style clasps; make beautiful, colorful beads that mimic real marble from pressed cotton balls and old nail polish; or create striking contemporary designs from simple cardboard.

As with all bracelets, consider the weight and overall balance of the bracelet when you design multistrand and linked bracelets. Use tiger tail and nylon line for simple strings of beads because they are strong and hard to break. Be careful to balance your design, making sure any central detail is positioned at the actual center of the bracelet. Check that repeated motifs and patterns use the same colors and are worked to the same size and tension. It is important that a bracelet is the right length; if it is too loose, it will continually catch on things and probably break; if it is too tight, it will affect your circulation and irritate your skin. To add a special finishing touch, include ornate clasps with several holes to join multiple threads. You can buy these from craft suppliers or hunt for authentic originals at antique fairs and rummage sales.

Once you have mastered the techniques in the step-by-step projects, you'll be ready to try the variations on each of the following designs. Use paper string instead of embroidery threads for an unusual linked bracelet. Experiment with different color combinations and sizes of beads to make new variations of the *Daisy Chain* design. Or use different paint techniques to give pressed cotton balls a special finish that imitates precious stones and minerals.

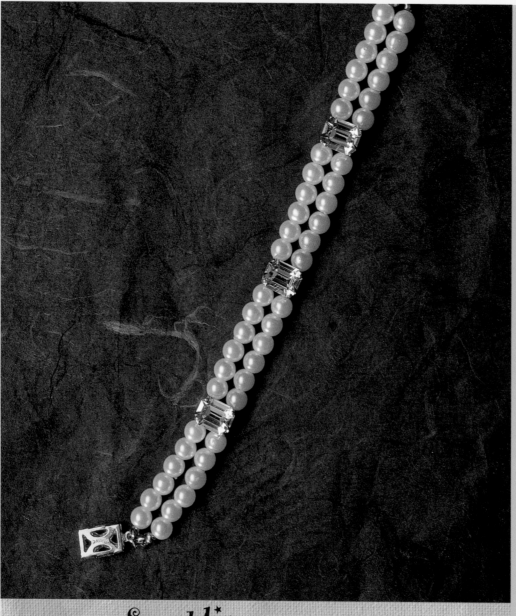

Sparkling
PEARLS

T HE DECADE OF THE 1930s WAS A GREAT ONE FOR creative jewelry design. Style books on this period or old fashion magazines are excellent sources of inspiration for your own individual creations. The 1930s-inspired bracelet in this project is simple yet stylish and worked in a combination of pearl beads and crystal stones. The sparkle from the diamond-like jewel stones makes this particular bead combination ideal for evenings, but the look of the bracelet can be totally transformed by choosing different colors, styles, and even sizes of beads. Pretty bracelets like these deserve to be finished off with attractive catches rather than plain bolt rings, but they shouldn't overpower the simplicity of the finished design. You can buy a variety of different styles from jewelry suppliers, but to discover more unusual and ornate designs, hunt for broken pieces of jewelry at an antiques fair or rummage sale.

You Will Need

Small pearl beads
3 glass-faceted jewelry stones and sewing mounts (with 4 holes)
Flat or needle-nosed pliers
Tiger tail, nylon, or strong cotton thread
2 calotte crimps
2 jump rings
Two-part clasp

Getting Started

Collect about 48 small pearl beads—the amount will vary, depending on the size of the beads and the finished length required. When working with jewelry stones, be careful not to scratch the stones with the pliers.

SPARKLING PEARLS

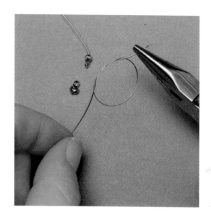

Cut 2 lengths of thread, each 6 inches / 15 cm longer than the required finished length. Make a knot in an end of each and neaten it with a calotte crimp.

Position the jewelry stones in their mounts, taking care to set them so they sit evenly. Squeeze the securing prongs down over the stone gently with flat or needle-nosed pliers, taking care not to damage the stone.

Start to string the beads onto the first thread, with 6 pearls followed by a jewel stone. Take the thread through 2 corresponding holes in the jewel stone.

Complete the first side, keeping the pattern regular and making sure all the jewel stones face the same way.

5. Double-check the length and make any adjustments to the pattern.

6. Work the second strand of the bracelet in the same way, taking it through the remaining 2 holes in the jewel stone.

7.

Twist open a jump ring and slip it through both loops on the calottes at an end of the bracelet and a loop on the clasp.

Close it securely by twisting the ends back together with pliers. Repeat at the opposite end to complete the bracelet.

Variations on a Theme

This 3-strand variation uses diamanté-encrusted spacer bars and a dramatic clasp to add detail to an otherwise simple design (right).

Experimenting with different-sized beads creates a more dramatic look (far right).

Harlequin
THREADS

Design Tips

Keep all embroidery thread to a reasonable length—anything 3 inches / 8 cm or more can be used—and sort them into color groups.

Look up different ideas on knotting, weaving, and braiding threads.

Experiment with jeweler's wire and pliers, and try making your own crimps if you can't find anything suitable for the materials you want to use.

You can cover piping cord with scraps of fabric for another look, or even paint fabric with your own design.

To give the threads a fine texture, string tiny beads onto embroidery thread and knot the thread on both sides of the bead to hold it in place.

Wire matching bought beads onto head pins and insert between calottes (instead of jump rings).

A BOX FULL OF COLORFUL EMBROIDERY THREADS inspired this unique bracelet. It is a wonderful way to use up thread left over from other projects. The design can be worked in endless color combinations, from the soft and subtle to contrasting, bright colors. The basic idea can be used in lots of other ways by varying the finding and what it is securing. For example, to change the look of this project the threads could be braided, woven, or knotted and even swapped with ribbons, fabrics, piping cord, fancy knitting yarns, or almost anything you can secure successfully in the finding. The findings themselves can be varied, too. Watch for different styles of crimps, especially those recommended for use with thicker threads, such as leather thong.

You Will Need

3 or 4 skeins of
cotton embroidery thread
Scissors
14 square calotte crimps
Clear-drying, all-purpose craft glue
Round- and needle-nosed pliers
8 jump rings
Clasp

Getting Started

Obtain about 14 square calotte crimps—the total number that you need will depend on your wrist measurement and the length of each thread link. To keep the threads taut as you twist them together, tie them to a door knob.

HARLEQUIN THREADS

1. Select the colors you want to incorporate in the link—the links can be all the same or each link can be worked with different color combinations.

2. Cut each thread to a length of approximately 18 inches / 46 cm, smooth them out, and lay them side by side.

3. Hold the threads tightly at one end or tie them to a door knob. Twist them together, working in the same direction all the time, until they are so tight they begin to buckle.

4. Fold the length of thread in half and let it twist around itself to form a cord. Working from the fold, insert the end of the cord into a square calotte crimp. Add a tiny blob of glue to the calotte before inserting the cord for added security. Use needle- or flat-nosed pliers to fold the edges of the crimp over the thread securely.

5.

Keeping the cord tightly twisted, place another square calotte crimp approximately 1 inch / 2.5 cm farther along the cord and secure as before. Keep the calotte seams facing in the same direction. Trim threads below the loop of each calotte with the tips of a sharp pair of scissors.

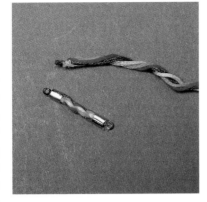

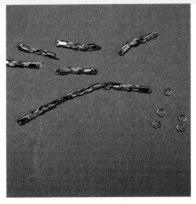

6.

Using pliers, twist open the jump rings and slip them through the loops on 2 calottes to join them together. Twist the ends of the rings back together to close.

7.

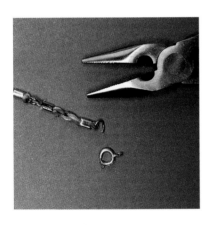

Join enough links to form a bracelet to fit comfortably around your wrist without falling off. Open up a jump ring and slip it through both the loop on a bolt ring clasp and the loop on the last calotte. Close to secure. Add a jump ring to the loop on the last calotte at the opposite end.

Variations on a Theme

Twisted paper giftwrap cord is cut into individual lengths, knotted, and made into a linked bracelet using square calotte crimps (right).

The velvet-covered piping cord shown here is just a single example of the different materials you can use to make this style of bracelet (far right).

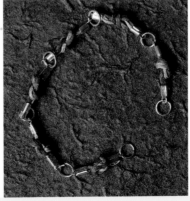

Daisy
CHAINS

THIS SIMPLE IDEA FOR A CHAIN OF FLOWERS IS easy to work and can be completely transformed by using different-sized beads and colors. Ideally the beads you choose should be smooth, like glass rocailles. This design is one of the easiest to master. If you are looking for more inspiration, look at illustrated books featuring the works of African tribal artisans or Native Americans. Or find a sourcebook on Victorian jewelry.

You Will Need

Black glass beads
Silver beads
Strong cotton thread or nylon line
Needle
2 calotte crimps
Clasp

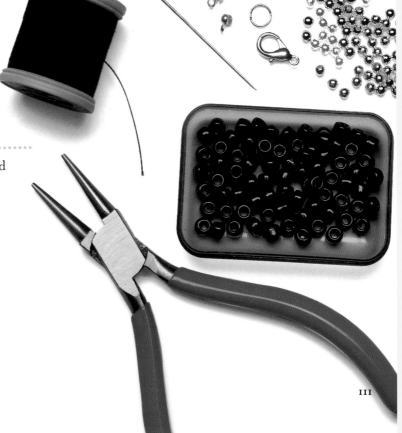

Getting Started

Cut two lengths of thread to the required finished length for your wrist plus 8 inches / 20 cm for knotting and threading. Obtain as many black glass beads and silver beads as you will need to make 6 or 7 flower shapes on the bracelet.

DAISY CHAINS

1.

Knot the ends of the threads together and secure the knot in the cup of a calotte crimp.

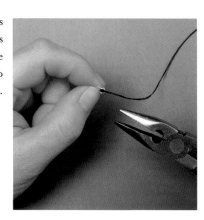

2.

Begin the design by threading on 3 silver beads.

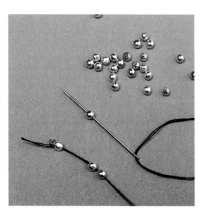

3.

Next, add 4 black beads.

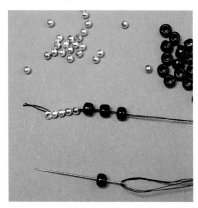

4.

Add a silver bead (this will be the center bead).

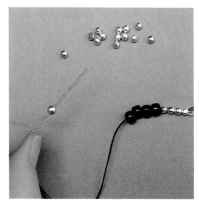

5.

Take the needle back through the first black bead.

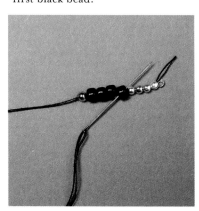

6.

Add 2 more black beads and take the needle through the fourth bead. Draw the thread up carefully and push the beads into shape.

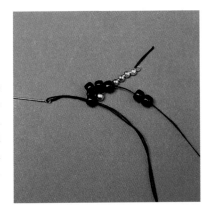

7.

Add 3 silver beads before working the next flower.

8.

When you have worked as many flowers as you need, finish with 3 silver beads and knot the thread close to the last bead. Enclose the knot in a calotte crimp, attach a clasp and jump ring to one end, and a single jump ring to the other end to complete the design.

Variations on a Theme

Larger beads in different colors give the same flower design a completely different look (right).

For a more delicate effect, weave tiny metallic beads in the same pattern (far right).

Button/Stud
EARRINGS

Earrings are one of the easiest types of jewelry to produce, and one of the simplest earring styles to make is basic button or stud shapes. Just visit your local jewelry, bead, and craft suppliers to find post, clip-on, or perforated fittings to which you can attach flat-backed cabochon stones or small faceted beads in jewel-bright colors. Slices cut from a wine bottle cork can be painted and beaded to make pretty earrings that bear no resemblance to their humble origins.

Consider the size of the earring design relative to your frame, hairstyle, and face shape—oversized earrings on a petite individual with a chic, gamine haircut look out of proportion and are better suited to taller people with bigger hairstyles. It is also important to position the earring back in the right place, whether it is close to the top of the earrings or with the post or clip dead center. If you have any doubts, use Blu Tak or plasticine to temporarily fix the finding and check in the mirror to see which position looks best. With abstract shapes, make sure the earrings face the same direction on each ear (in mirror images of each other) before permanently fixing the finding in place.

It's easy to reinterpret any of the designs that follow. Cork slices can be painted in any color and decorated with beaded pins, metal spirals, or ornate hand-painted designs. Fabric paints and pens come in such a wide range of colors that they are perfect for experimenting with different pattern ideas, from defined geometric designs to free-flowing, unstructured variations. Abstract papier-mâché shapes provide a great base for intricate hand-painted designs, but they look just as good in plain colors with glamorous jewel stones adding a touch of sparkle.

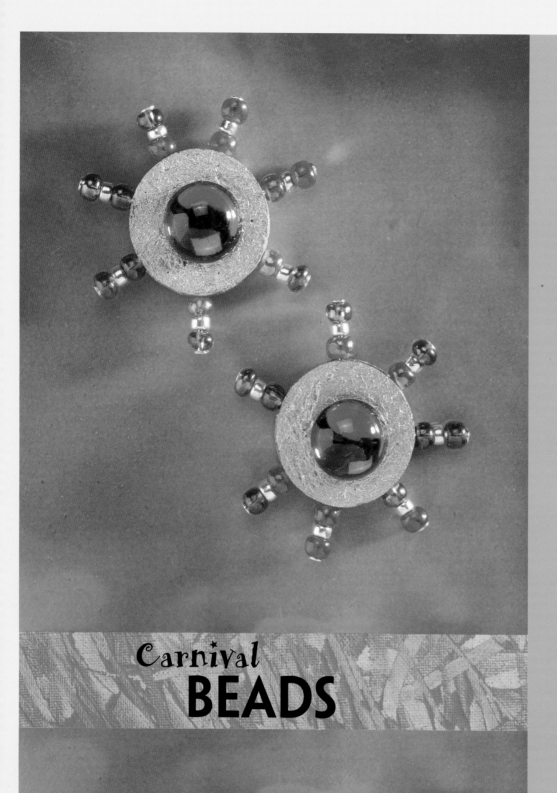

Carnival
BEADS

Design Tips

Decorate the cork center with a more intricate painted design and bead the pins with coordinating colors.

To create a spider-web effect, weave colored embroidery threads or jewelry wire in and out of the pins.

For a totally natural look leave the cork unpainted. Just smooth the surface with an emery board and, making sure it is dust-free, add several coats of varnish to bring out the grain.

Decorate pins with wooden beads to complement the natural look of the cork.

Once you have mastered the art of making metal spirals, try winding them out from a small bead center.

Instead of gluing one striking central bead to the cork, try adding lots of tiny stones at random for a jewel-encrusted finish; then add coordinating bead pins.

MAKING SOMETHING FROM NOTHING IS A REALLY rewarding hobby and once you get started, you'll find potential in the most unusual objects and delight friends with your creativity. It is surprisingly easy disguising the origins of everyday materials to produce stylish pieces of jewelry. These imaginative earrings are made from slices cut off an ordinary wine bottle cork that are then cleverly transformed with a coat of metallic paint and bead decoration. Cork is a particularly versatile material to work with; you can easily paint it and insert beads on pins into it. The ideas illustrated require no special skills or equipment and can be made in a very short time. Use the designs for inspiration to create your own unique interpretations.

Getting Started

Sterilize the cork before you start the project using household bleach or a sterilizing solution from your local pharmacy. Make sure you use clear-drying glue that is suitable for all surfaces.

You Will Need

A cork
Sterilizing solution or bleach
Cutting mat
Craft knife
Emery board
Gesso
Paintbrush
Gold metallic paint
Darning needle or large
tapestry needle
Varnish (optional)
14 head pins
A selection of beads
Wire cutters
Clear-drying hobby adhesive
Epoxy or similar strong adhesive
2 flat-backed jewel stones
2 ear clip findings
(or studs if preferred)

CARNIVAL BEADS

1. When the sterilized cork is completely dry, cut 2 slices approximately ¼ inch / .5 cm thick using a heavy-duty craft knife.

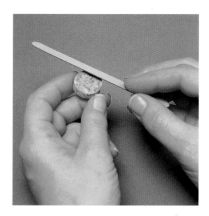

2. Smooth the surface with an emery board. Brush off any dust residue.

3. Paint all surfaces with a gesso undercoat. Let dry and then add a coat of gold metallic paint.

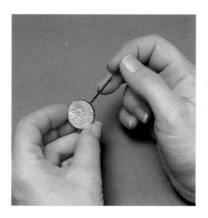

4. Use a thick needle to pierce 7 holes at regular intervals around the edge of the slice. Varnish at this stage if required.

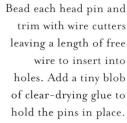

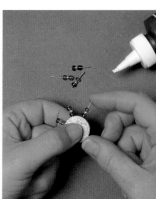

5. Bead each head pin and trim with wire cutters leaving a length of free wire to insert into holes. Add a tiny blob of clear-drying glue to hold the pins in place.

Variations on a Theme

SILVER SPIRALS

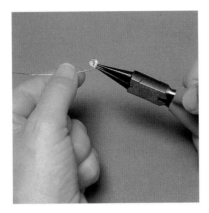

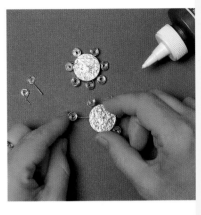

6.

Glue central stones and earring backs in place with the stronger adhesive.

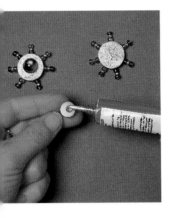

1.

Metal spirals are easy to make and give the cork slices a completely different look. Cut a length of jeweler's wire and, with the tip of the pliers, start the spiral by turning a small loop at the end. Wind the wire around the loop until the spiral is the size you want.

Make holes in the side edge of a painted cork slice as in step 4 above. Insert the spirals, the tips marked with a blob of glue to secure.

3.

Finish with either a clip-on or stud earring back.

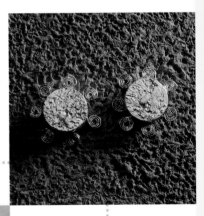

For this variation the cork has been painted black and 8 pins beaded with a single black bead. This idea would also look good with a black center and white beads, or vice versa (right).

Design Tips

Sketch out your design on paper first and fill in colors with crayons or paints that match your fabric paints.

Experiment with different textile techniques like tie-dye or batik to create more interesting finishes.

Back a piece of silky fabric with iron-on interfacing to lend it more substance and to make it easier to fashion into different earring shapes.

Mount the finished design on cardboard or use self-cover buttons.

Experiment with the many textured fabric paints available to create different effects.

Pastel Checkerboard
BUTTONS

FABRIC PAINTING IS A WONDERFUL way to decorate all kinds of textiles and allows you to be totally creative and experimental. The project shown here is simple to work and is designed to inspire you to create your own patterns. The simple geometric design is worked out on paper first and then used as a template. Fabric-painting pens add the color; these are just like felt-tipped pens and give you greater control over where they are placed. To prevent the colors from bleeding into one another, use a special outline resist called gutta, which is also used to outline the design before the color is added. You can buy gutta in lots of different colors including clear, which can be washed out. Fabric paints come in pots just like ordinary paints and are applied with a brush. The colors, which can be fixed with a warm iron, are completely washable.

Getting Started

Cut the silky fabric into a square. (If you want paler finishes, use a synthetic fabric.) Choose a color of gutta that complements the color of the fabric pens you will use. A pearlized gutta was used in this project to highlight the pretty pastel shades.

You Will Need

Cardboard
2 self-cover buttons
Pencil
Ruler
Tracing paper
Silky fabric
Embroidery hoop
Adhesive tape
Gutta and fabric painting pens
Iron-on interfacing
Compass
Scissors
Needle
Thread
2 earring backs
(clip-on or post fittings)
All-purpose craft glue

PASTEL CHECKERBOARD BUTTONS

1.

Place the button base on cardboard and draw around its circum-ference to get the area of the finished design.

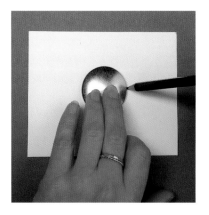

2.

Draw the outline of the pattern or motif on the cardboard and transfer to tracing paper.

3.

Fix the fabric in an embroidery hoop and tape the motif to the wrong side. Make sure the fabric is taut.

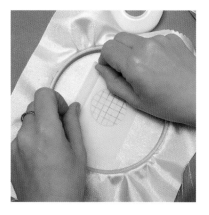

4.

Test the gutta on a fabric scrap to get the feel of the paint flow, then outline the pattern or motif and let dry. Fill in the colors, being careful not to mark the gutta. Do a test piece before starting on the real thing.

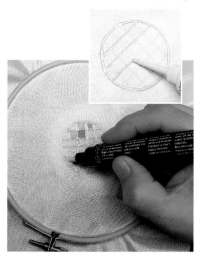

5.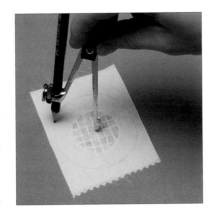

Remove the painted design from the hoop and trim the fabric, leaving at least 1 inch / 2.5 cm all around. Iron the interfacing to the wrong side (to fix the colors) and draw a larger circle to the size indicated on the button cardboard.

6.

Use pliers to remove the button shank. Then run a gathering thread close to the edge of the outer circle. Place the button in the center of your design and draw up the thread, easing the fabric over the serrated edge.

7.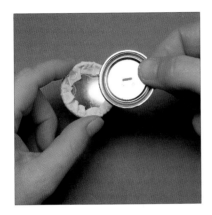

Clip on the back to hold the fabric secure and glue an earring back in place.

Variations on a Theme

This design was achieved by painting the fabric. The first coat was applied with a water-laden brush. Then pink and gold highlights were applied using a fairly dry brush. Let each coat dry before applying the next (right).

Textured paint in a vividly contrasting color was used to add polka-dots to the same painted base used for the previous variation (far right).

123

Tivoli Lights Sunburst
EARRINGS

THE FABULOUS VARIETY OF BEADS AVAILABLE
in myriad colors is inspiration on its own; it is almost
impossible to choose just a small selection. A
jar of faceted glass beads in a mix of sizes and a kaleidoscopic
range of colors is the inspiration for these ornately beaded
earrings. They are much simpler to make than they look and use
a clever perforated back that allows you to sew thread in and out.
This is then clipped to an earring back to complete the design.
The tassels are a dramatic touch but the basic style of these
earrings has been around for centuries. When working with
such an eclectic mix of colors, it doesn't matter if
each earring in the pair is slightly different as long as
the overall balance of color is the same. Points of
interest, like the tassels, however, are likely to draw
more attention and it is best if these are identical on each.

Getting Started

Allocate 30 to 35 small, faceted beads and 30 to 35 stopper beads for each
earring. The stopper beads, when threaded with the larger beads, secure
the larger bead onto the earring fitting. Cut a length of thread approximately 30 inches / 76 cm long. (You may prefer to work on shorter
lengths and oversew to tie off each end before starting on the next.)

You Will Need

60 to 70 small faceted beads
6 larger beads for tassel ends
60 to 70 stopper beads
Invisible thread or fine nylon line
Beading needle
2 perforated earring
fittings with backs
Glue
Pliers

TIVOLI LIGHTS SUNBURST EARRINGS

1. Make a large knot in the end of the thread. Take it through the center hole of the perforated fitting from the concave side and add the first bead and stopper bead.

2. Take the needle around the stopper bead and back through the first bead.

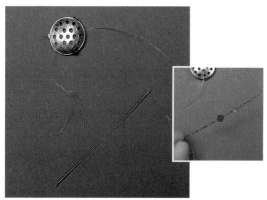

3. Bring the needle back through the center hole and through the center of the knot to secure.

Bring the needle back to the right side through a hole adjacent to the center point. Add a bead and stopper bead as before and take the needle back to the wrong side. Working in circles following the pierced holes on the perforated fitting, continue in the same way until you have completed the outside edge. Depending on the size of your beads, it may not be necessary to bead every hole—you will have to judge this as you go. Oversew the end of the last thread, working the stitches in and out of the holes on the perforated fitting.

5.

Position the tassels between 2 claws on the perforated fitting to allow enough room to clamp the claws over the earring back. Make a large knot in a piece of thread 12 inches / 30.5 cm long. Thread the needle through the back from the wrong side and add enough beads to make the first tassel. End with a larger bead and stopper bead. Take the thread back through all but the stopper bead and secure on the wrong side. Work the other tassels on both sides in the same way.

6.

Add a dab of glue to all knots and loose ends as a precaution.

7.

Clamp the claws of the perforated fitting over the earring back using pliers.

Variations on a Theme

The same techniques are used to create monochromatic earrings from faceted glass beads (right).

Try beading pearls and crystals onto a perforated fitting to create an elegant pair of earrings (far right).

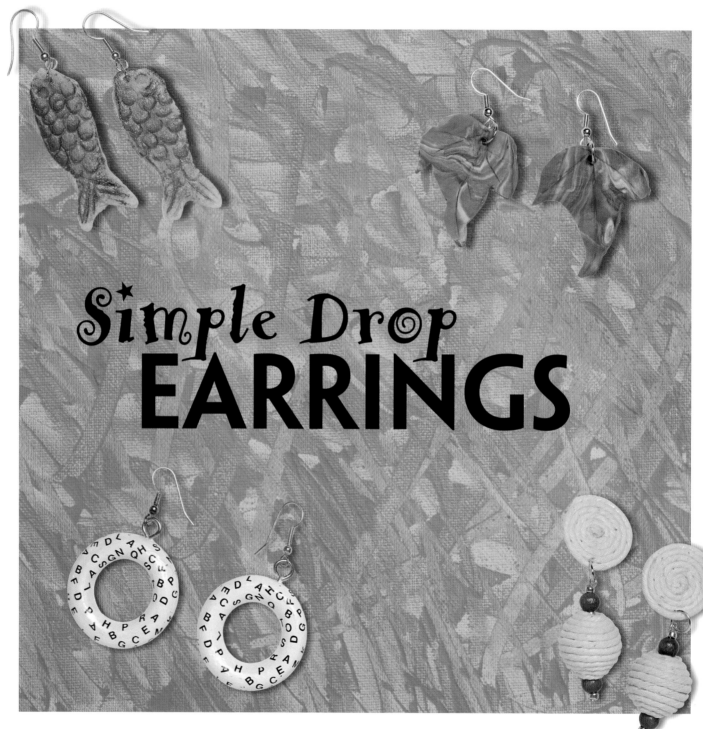

Simple Drop EARRINGS

There is a seemingly infinite variety of simple drop earring styles available, along with an extensive range of findings to make assembling them a simple task. You can choose hoops in different shapes that can be bought ready-formed for instant beading, or make your own from jeweler's wire shaped around a piece of dowel, a broom handle, or bead container. Ear studs, hooks, kidney wires, and a variety of screw fastenings and clip-on findings come with integral loops to make joining simple drops easy, and all are readily available from craft, bead, and jewelry specialists.

You can make drops and tops from all kinds of materials. The most traditional styles use beads that can be threaded in attractive groups onto hoops and head pins, or linked together individually with eye pins. Head and eye pins are joined directly or with jump rings to the loop on an earring finding or top of your choice. You can also make charms to use as drops from other elements like pewter, salt dough, and polymer modeling clays or create fun variations of the classic hoop style from ordinary wooden curtain rings. Make sure that the drops hang correctly when using other elements; sometimes you will need to use more than one jump ring to ensure the charm faces the right direction.

Use the main step-by-step project for inspiration on related designs. By using modeling clays in different colors, you can transform spring leaves into autumn leaves. By wrapping beads in attractive metal cages instead of string, you can create a more sophisticated look.

Take the time to practice turning perfect loops on head pins since this can affect how the drop falls.

Vary the size and shape of beads to create different visual effects.

To prevent the head pin slipping through larger beads, use a tiny rocaille as a stopper bead.

When making your own hoops, wrap the beaded wire around a tube to shape the curve—the tubes that hold small beads are ideal.

Hoops in different shapes and sizes can be bought from jewelry suppliers and all you need to do is add the beads you want.

Beaded
HOOPS

J UST A FEW BEADS, THE MOST BASIC FINDINGS, and tools are all that's needed to create sensational dangle earrings in minutes. These designs illustrate the basic techniques involved, and once you have mastered them you will find yourself thinking up lots of your own variations. Most of these ideas work best with bought beads but you could mix them with your own papier-mâché or clay designs to add your own personal touch. Look for bead supplier catalogs that not only illustrate the fantastic variety of shapes, sizes, and colors available, but will also provide you with endless inspiration for different bead combinations. Choose beads in colors to match an outfit, an occasion, or simply your mood—crystal, jet, and diamanté instantly add a touch of glamour for evenings; brighter colors in clashing combinations look fun and funky; pearls mixed with almost anything look elegant and classy.

Getting Started

Each of these pairs of simple drop earrings use a different method to dangle beautiful beads. An ear wire is an uncomplicated way to gather a beaded hoop or to hang a head pin stacked with contrasting small and large beads. Use triangle bails to dangle crystal drops from ear clips decorated with cabochon stones.

You Will Need

FOR THE BEADED HOOPS
Jeweler's wire
Wire cutters
Pliers
Glass rocaille beads
2 jump rings
2 ear wires

FOR THE PEARL AND
BLUE GLASS BEAD DROPS
6 small pearls
2 larger beads in a contrasting color
2 head pins
Wire cutters
Pliers
2 ear wires

FOR CABOCHON AND
CRYSTAL DROPS
2 ear clips with integral loops
2 flat-backed cabochon stones
2 crystal drop beads
Epoxy glue
2 triangle bails
pliers

131

BEADED HOOPS

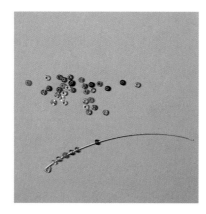

1.

Cut a piece of wire
approximately 3 inches /
7.5 cm long, turn a small
loop at one end with
pliers, and thread on
beads from the other end.

2.

Leave enough room to
turn a loop at the
opposite end.

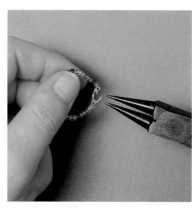

3.

Use pliers to open up a
jump ring and slip it
through both loops to
form a circle of beads.

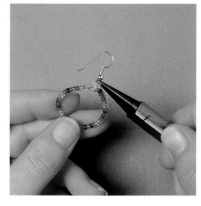

4.

Open up the loop at the
base of an ear wire with
pliers. Slip the jump
ring of the bead hoop
into the loop and close
the loop to secure.

Variations on a Theme

PEARL & BLUE GLASS DROPS

1. Thread the beads onto a head pin—the head of the pin will prevent the beads from falling off. Trim the pin with cutters, leaving enough to turn a loop using pliers.

2. Open up the loop at the base of an ear wire with pliers. Slip the loop at the top of the head pin into the loop.

CABOCHON & CRYSTAL DROPS

1. Glue the cabochon to the ear clip, making sure the integral loop is not obscured. Let dry completely.

2. Open up the triangle bail and slip it through the loop on the ear clip. Position the hole at the top of the crystal drop between the two sides of the triangle.

3. Close up the loop to secure and complete the earrings.

3. Close securely with pliers to complete the earrings.

Jeweled Punched Tin
DANGLES

Experiment with different shapes. A square is easy to begin with but the options are endless: flowers, fish, and hearts are just a few examples.

Treat the metal like fabric and clip into curves to turn under edges. On intricate shapes this may be impossible, so smooth edges with a fine metal file.

If your design feels flimsy and is easily bent out of shape, back it with a piece of suede, leather, or thick cardboard.

Punching a design is only one idea. The metal is so soft you can also work relief designs.

Pewter is not the only metal you can use. It is possible to buy copper, tin, and aluminum in sheets. You can also recycle household cans as long as they aren't too thick—traditional square olive oil cans are ideal, as are aluminum soft drink cans. (In the case of round cans, wash, dry, and lay the metal out flat under something heavy.)

WORKING WITH METAL IS A DAUNTING THOUGHT for many people since it is often assumed that special skills or expensive equipment is required. A great deal depends on the metal you choose to work with. The sheet pewter used for this project couldn't be easier to use since it is a soft metal that can be cut and shaped like fabric using heavy-duty scissors or a craft knife. This design is simple to produce, but once you gain a little experience and get used to the feel of the metal, it can be used to create very special pieces of jewelry. Pewterwork is a popular craft on its own. To find inspiration for more complicated designs, consult the many books and manuals that illustrate all the different techniques.

You Will Need

A small piece of sheet pewter
Cutting mat
Ballpoint pen
Steel ruler
Scissors
Darning needle
Small hammer
Panel pin
Piece of board
2 jewel stones
Epoxy or cement glue
Jump rings
2 eye pins or head pins
Coordinating beads
2 earring wires

Getting Started

You can use a pair of scissors to cut thin metal, but beware—the metal will blunt the cutting edge of the scissors. Try tin cutters to snip through thicker metals. For best results when cutting the metal, work on an old cutting board.

135

JEWELED PUNCHED TIN DANGLES

1. Place the metal sheet on top of a cutting mat and use a ballpoint pen and a steel ruler to draw a square, ¾ inch / 2 cm wide, then a border within that square ¼ inch / .5 cm wide. Press down firmly with the pen to indent the metal.

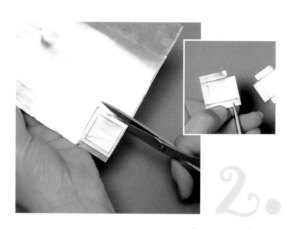

2. Cut out each shape cleanly, cutting along the border edges. Cut out tiny squares in each corner as illustrated using the tips of your scissors.

3. Fold over the border edges along the indented lines to enclose the pen lines. Trim corners to neaten if necessary.

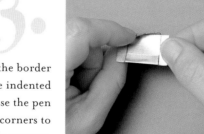

4. With the cutting mat on top of a piece of board, mark the outline of the punched design with the tip of a darning needle, making light indentations. Placing the point of the panel pin over an indentation, hammer out the design, piercing the metal.

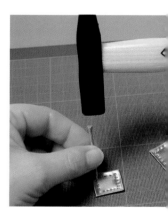

5.

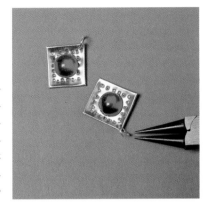

Use the hammer and panel pin to make a hole in a corner of each square. Glue jewel stones in place and let dry completely. Open up a jump ring and slip through each hole.

6.

Snip the head end off a head pin and turn a loop using pliers. Insert the jump ring through the loop and close it securely. Add beads in the required order, trim the head pin using wire cutters, leaving enough length to turn another loop.

7.

Open up the loop at the base of an ear wire using pliers and slip it through the loop on the head pin. Close it again to secure.

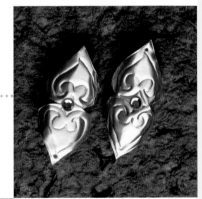

Variations on a Theme

A shell quilting pattern inspired the design for these pretty copper earrings. The motif was drawn to size on tracing paper and then the outline followed with the point of a knitting needle. Work on top of a wad of newspaper to get better relief (right).

This motif was inspired by a heraldic coat of arms (far right).

Ivy LEAVES

Design Tips

To get the best finish with polymer modeling clays, knead them well to soften and remove any air bubbles. This should then create a smooth surface when the clay is rolled out.

Leave the clay wrapped in a plastic bag on top of a towel on a warm radiator to speed up the softening time. Or buy special preparations produced by the manufacturers that do the same job.

Practice getting the perfect marbled effect by working with small pieces of clay before beginning the actual project.

When you've mastered the technique you can move on to experiment with other, more complicated color combinations.

Experiment with different shapes of leaves and marbled effects— browns and reds can be used to give a feel of autumn.

ODAY'S SYNTHETIC MODELING CLAYS ARE A WONDER-
fully versatile modeling medium for craft jewelry designers
to work with. They are soft and malleable, and once the
clay has been kneaded and warmed in your hands, it is simple to
sculpt, mold, or cut into a variety of shapes. The range of available colors is extensive and can be used on their own or blended
together to create spectacular marbled effects. Rolled out like
pastry, the clay is ideal for using with cookie cutters, cardboard
templates, and found objects like the leaves that inspired these
pretty earrings. The clay is so soft it is possible to imprint the
shape of a leaf and its veins, which is then cut out with a craft
knife. Two of the greatest advantages these polymer clays have
over traditional cold clays is that they set hard quickly in a
low-temperature domestic oven and won't shatter if
dropped. A coat of varnish increases the depth of the colors and produces a finish similar to kiln-fired ceramics.

Getting Started

Knead the Fimo with your thumbs and fingers until very soft
and pliable. This will make it much easier to roll and will prevent cracks. Wash your hands when changing colors to prevent one
rubbing off on the other and spoiling the finished effect.

You Will Need

2 blocks of Fimo,
1 white and 1 green
Rolling pin
1 or 2 fallen ivy leaves
Craft knife
Thick needle
2 jump rings
2 ear hooks
Varnish
Paintbrush
Pliers

IVY LEAVES

1.

Break off a piece of Fimo from each block, knead, and roll out into log shapes. Wrap the 2 colors around each other and roll again to form a single log shape. Fold this in half, twist the 2 halves together and knead to blend the colors together. Continue twisting and kneading until you get a marbled effect.

2.

Roll the clay out like pastry on a flat surface to a thickness of approximately ¼ inch / .5 cm.

3.

Place leaves on top of Fimo with the vein side directly on the clay.

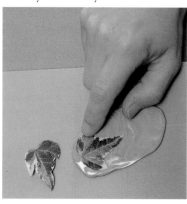

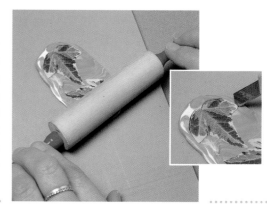

4.

To get a deeper impression use a rolling pin to press the leaves into the clay. Very carefully cut out around the outline of each leaf using a craft knife. Give the edges of each leaf as much detail as possible.

5.

Use a needle to pierce a hole at the stalk end of each leaf to attach the ear fitting, then fire in a low-temperature oven as recommended on the packet instructions.

6.

Twist open the jump rings and insert through the pierced holes and the loop at the bottom of any ear hook. Close the jump rings securely using pliers.

7.

Paint each leaf with a few coats of varnish to give depth to the marbled colors.

Variations on a Theme

For a striking autumnal feel, select different leaf shapes and change the colors used to marble the clay to red and brown (right).

More stylized leaf shapes can be cut from plain Fimo using a cardboard template and craft knife (far right).

141

Multidrop & Linked EARRINGS

The same basic techniques described to make simple drop earrings can be extended to make more extravagant drop and link designs. Use more than one drop, vary the lengths of the strand, join and link several of the same elements together, and vary the color combinations. Look for decorative spacers, ear and necklace hangers, necklace ends, bead cups, bell caps, and even clasps to create wonderfully original earrings. Try adding buttons, sequins, and even children's tiddly-winks to enrich your designs. Sequins come in all shapes and sizes and have the advantage of being as light as a feather. You can also make your own earrings from polymer clays, air-dry clays, and papier-mâché shapes. What you choose to use depends on the style of the earrings, whether they are clip-on, post and butterfly, or hook fittings.

As you develop your multidrop designs, it is important to create a balanced, completed design that won't overpower the shape of your face or get lost in your hairstyle. If you use more than one strand, make sure the earrings hang correctly. The design should be perfectly balanced so it doesn't tilt to one side. You may need to use more than one jump ring to ensure the drop or charm faces the right direction. These are things that come with practice and are possible to correct if you don't get it right the first time.

Feel free to experiment with techniques and materials to create variations on the projects shown here. For example, by swapping paper for textured paint, papier-mâché earring bases are completely transformed. Try using different cutters or paint effects on air-dry clay to increase the design options tenfold.

Shades of Blue
EARRINGS

Design Tips

Sketch out design ideas on paper to experiment with different color combinations and sizes and shapes of beads.

It is important to get the strands to balance correctly or the earrings will look lopsided.

Vary the number and length of the bead strands to create different effects.

One single strand of large beads can look quite dramatic hung from the center hole.

Experiment with different styles and shapes of bell caps. Fluted bell caps conceal the connection between the top of the beaded strands, making it look like a beaded tassel.

THE FILIGREE BELL CAPS USED TO MAKE THESE earrings are just one of the many decorative findings available and are multipurpose, too. Here they are used to dangle bead strands, but they can also be used on both sides of a bead to make it look more special or to begin and end a necklace or bracelet. The ready-made holes around the edges are perfect for joining bead strands using a jump ring. The central hole can be wired with a longer strand and provide the link for an ear wire. This style of earring can be bold and striking or pretty and delicate, depending on the size of the bell cap and the beads used for the dangles.

You Will Need

2 filigree bell caps
Beads
Eye pins
Wire cutters
Pliers
2 ear wires
Jump rings

Getting Started

Select beads in several shades of the same color and in a few varied sizes. Remember that you don't have to thread bead strands through all of the holes on the filigree bell caps; this project uses only 4 strands per earring.

SHADES OF BLUE EARRINGS

Thread the beads in groups or singularly onto an eye pin.

2.

Trim the pin, leaving enough wire to turn another loop.

3.

To make the strands, open up a jump ring and slip through the loops of 2 beaded pins. Close the ring securely. Join as many beaded pins together as necessary to get the length required.

4.

Open up the jump rings and slip through the holes around the end of the bell cap.

5.

Before closing the ring, slip it through the loop at the end of a bead strand, then close securely.

6.

Add as many strands as you wish to the edge of the bell cap, then insert an eye pin through the central hole so that the preformed loop sits on top of the cap. Trim the pin and turn a loop at the other end.

7.

Join the central strand to the last loop with a jump ring. Close securely.

8.

To complete the earrings, open up the loop at the bottom of an ear wire and slip through the central loop on the top of the bell cap. Close securely.

Variations on a Theme

These triangles have predrilled holes along the bottom edge and top point of the triangle. Beads have been wired onto head pins and linked to the finding with jump rings (right).

The striking copper hanger that forms the base for these earrings was taken from a broken necklace. Rocaille beads have been threaded onto head pins and linked to the hanger with jump rings (far right).

147

Design Tips

Make a sketch of your design idea before starting, work out the colors and sizes, and then count to make sure you have enough buttons.

Use larger buttons for the legs to give the impression of trousers and work the body and arms in the same color to look like a sweater.

Use strong cotton or invisible thread to work the design.

Make sure both legs and both arms are strung with the identical buttons, in the same order.

Try making your own buttons with polymer clays or air-dry clays.

Button People
EARRINGS

USING BUTTONS AS FASTENINGS ON CLOTHES IS NOT the only way to admire their beauty, color, and shape. They can also be linked and strung together like beads to make innovative jewelry designs. Lots of people have wonderful collections of buttons that never see the light of day and these whimsical earrings are the perfect way to show them off. It is simply the way they are strung together that creates the effect of arms, legs, and bodies. Once you have mastered the basic button technique, you can have fun giving the button people individual characteristics and use buttons in different colors to give them the appearance of wearing trousers and a top. Glue larger buttons at different angles to give the idea of a jaunty hat. Keep both sides of the design the same and choose buttons of similar sizes to create a balanced look overall.

You Will Need

20 to 28 buttons for 4 arms
20 to 28 buttons for 4 legs
6 to 10 larger buttons for bodies
2 to 4 buttons for necks
2 buttons for hats
8 small beads for hands and feet
2 larger beads for heads
Strong cotton or invisible thread
Needle
2 ear hooks
All-purpose clear-drying glue

Getting Started

Cut 2 lengths of thread, each approximately 18 inches / 46 cm long. The small beads, which will look like hands and feet, will act like stopper beads for the buttons on the arms and legs.

BUTTON PEOPLE EARRINGS

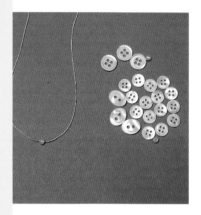

1. Fold a length of thread in half and insert one end through the hole in a small bead.

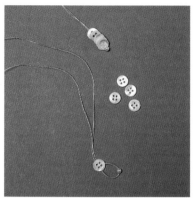

2. To make a leg, take one end of the length of thread through a hole in a button and take the other end through a hole directly opposite the first. Repeat. Make the other leg in the same way.

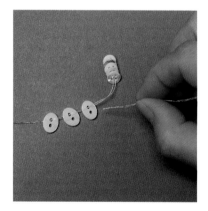

3. Take both ends of thread from a leg and insert through the same hole on a larger button for the body. Add 2 or 3 buttons as required. Insert both ends of thread from the second leg through an opposite hole.

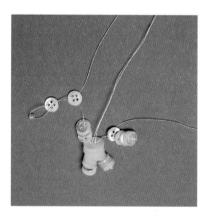

4. To make an arm, separate the pair of threads on one side and take only one through a hole in each button. When the arm is long enough, push the thread through a small bead and then back up the arm through the holes directly opposite the first. Work the other arm in the same way.

5.

Add 1 or 2 buttons to make the neck, threading buttons onto the thread as for the body. Insert all ends of thread through a bead to make the "head."

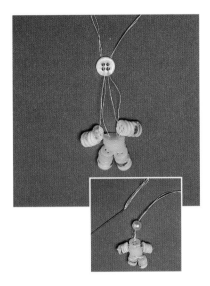

6.

Add a button to make a hat, taking the threads through a hole and back through the opposite. Secure the thread with a knot and a dab of glue.

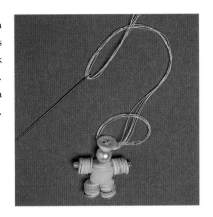

7.

Twist open the loop at the bottom of an earring hook and push it under the threads on the hat. Close to secure.

Variations on a Theme

Horn and mother-of-pearl buttons are combined with wooden beads in this alternative (right).

A collection of pretty pastel buttons has been mixed with transparent buttons and blue beads to create this effect (far right).

Hearts of GOLD

T

HESE PRETTY HEART earrings were inspired by a Coco Chanel design that appeared in *Vogue* magazine. The new design is interpreted in a slightly different way and doesn't contain all the elements of the original, but the earrings still look stylish and chic. They are easy to make from a modern air-dry clay that gives a wonderful ceramic finish without the need for an expensive kiln. Painted with special cold ceramic paints, air-dry clay really does mimic china and porcelain. It is easy to mold, sculpt, and cut just like polymer clays and can be substituted for all the projects that don't rely on the poly clay colors (you won't get the same marbled or millefiori effects even with clever paint techniques).

Getting Started

After you cut out the heart shapes from the clay, smooth their edges with a damp paintbrush or your fingers. Wait to trim the eye pins that are inserted into the hearts until after you paint the piece—the length of the pins makes the hearts easier to paint.

You Will Need

Air-dry clay
Rolling pin
Heart-shaped cutters in small and medium sizes
8 eye pins
Wire cutters
Superglue
Artist's gesso
Paintbrush
Red acrylic enamel paint
Gold Plaka paint
Chain
10 jump rings
Pliers
2 earring backs
(clip-on or post fittings)

HEARTS OF GOLD

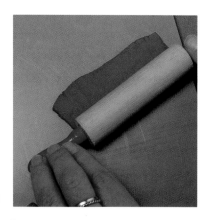

Roll out the clay on a flat surface to a thickness of approximately ¼ inch / .5 cm.

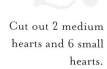

Cut out 2 medium hearts and 6 small hearts.

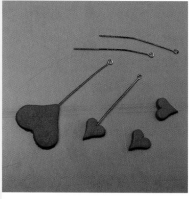

Insert an eye pin ¼ inch / .5 cm into the clay at the bottom of the 2 larger hearts and at the top of the 6 small hearts. Leave them until they set hard, with no signs of moisture.

Paint each heart with gesso. When dry, gently ease the eye pins out from the clay, trim so that only the eye extends beyond the clay and insert them back in the holes. Use a dab of superglue to secure them in place.

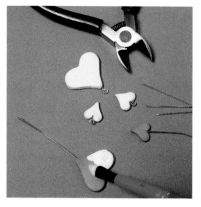

Paint both sides of the small hearts gold and the larger hearts red. Let dry.

6. Divide the chain into 3 different lengths for each earring, snipping the links with wire cutters.

7. Slip the top link of each chain onto a jump ring. Attach a small heart to the bottom of each chain with a jump ring slipped through the last chain link and the eye on the heart. Join the heart drops to the ear-ring top with a jump ring inserted through the eye on the main heart and the jump ring at the top of the drop.

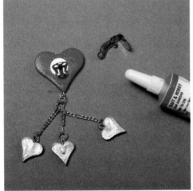

8. Glue an earring back to the reverse side of the top heart.

Variations on a Theme

Stars and moons are a celestial combination that always works well. The clay motifs shown here have been painted silver and linked together with a crystal bead (right).

Air-dry clay provides a wonderful base for paint techniques as these oak leaf and acorn earrings illustrate (far right).

Badge-Style
PINS

Pins have been used in both functional and decorative forms for thousands of years. The ancient Greeks fastened the shoulders of their *peplos,* or outer garments, with open pins with decorated heads. These were later replaced by more substantial *fibulae,* or brooches.

Badge-style pins, one of the easiest pieces of jewelry to make, are still a great way of holding scarves in place or for dressing up a plain outfit. This style has no dangles and is turned into a pin by simply gluing or sewing a flat metal bar with a pin and catch to the back of a plain metal disc. Pin backs and plain metal discs are available from jewelry, bead, and craft suppliers. You can also buy perforated fittings with claws that will clamp over the metal base plates, making it easy to sew on ornate beads or decorative buttons.

Many kinds of materials—from traditional beads and jewel stones to craft rubber and sheet metals—can be added for exciting effects. Dazzling jewel stones set in mounts look wonderful glued together in the shape of a cross; ordinary metal hexagonal nuts fit

together to make a flower-shaped pin that looks sensational decorated with flat-backed jewels. Fine sheet metals like pewter, copper, and aluminum are easy to cut and shape with tin cutters or a craft knife and can be given a pierced Shaker design or a relief pattern taken from ancient artifacts.

Linen & Button
SAMPLER

Design Tips

Sketch out different brooch shapes and think of some alternative decorating ideas—tiny jewel stones or beads will add a touch of sparkle, light dabs of gold paint will produce a more baroque look.

Experiment with different amounts of PVA glue until you achieve the desired effect.

Experiment with different fabrics— some will work better than others. As a general rule, avoid anything that is too thick, like corduroy.

Try adding a more textured effect by pleating, gathering, or folding the fabric origami-style before painting with PVA.

Keeping to the sampler theme, try stitching a miniature traditional-style sampler before stiffening.

A SAMPLER BROOCH PROVIDES THE PERFECT BASE FOR displaying a collection of beautiful buttons or other precious objects. Its soft, flexible appearance is deceptive—it is in fact rigid and therefore more durable than an ordinary piece of fabric. Stiffening fabric is very easy and opens up a world of new ideas for using it as jewelry-making material. There are several ways to stiffen fabric, but one of the easiest is simply to apply a coat of clear-drying PVA glue. When dry, it leaves a transparent plastic-like coating on the fabric. Pleats, gathers, and folds can be made permanent, creating interesting sculptural effects. The basic idea can be applied to a wide range of fabrics from silk to lace and an infinite variety of shapes to suit your personal style, outfit, or occasion.

You Will Need

Piece of linen
Scissors
PVA glue
Paintbrush
Ceramic plate
Toothpick
Tailor's chalk
Selection of buttons
Coordinating embroidery thread
Small tapestry needle
All-purpose, clear-drying glue
Pin back

Getting Started

For this pin, you will need a piece of linen 1½ inches / 3.8 cm square. When gluing the fabric, turn it over several times while it is drying, or else it may stick to the plate and be pulled out of shape when removed.

159

LINEN & BUTTON SAMPLER

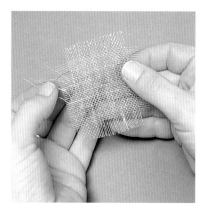

Carefully fray the edges of the linen square evenly all around to leave a central area of fabric approximately 1 inch / 2.5 cm square.

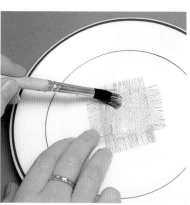

Lay the fabric out flat on a ceramic plate and apply an even coat of PVA glue, including the frayed edges.

Use a toothpick to tease the frayed edges back into shape, then let dry. Turn the fabric over before it's completely dry to help prevent it from sticking to the plate. Use the tips of a pair of scissors to separate the frayed edges if necessary.

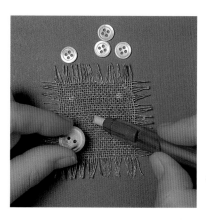

Lay the buttons on the fabric and work out your design. Mark their final positions with tailor's chalk.

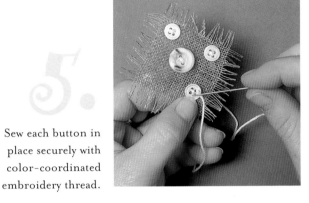

5.

Sew each button in place securely with color-coordinated embroidery thread.

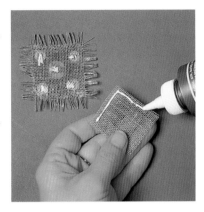

6.

Cut out a square of linen, 1 inch / 2.5 cm, to use as a backing and glue it in place to cover any knots or ugly threads on the back of the sampler.

7.

Glue a pin back in position and let dry completely.

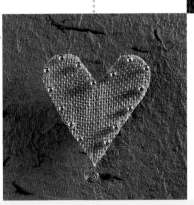

Variations on a Theme

The stiffened fabric in this variation (right) has been used to create a sharper, more sophisticated shape. Tiny gold beads outline the heart and a decorative metal spiral adds the perfect finishing touch.

A pleated strip of dark blue silk, stiffened with PVA glue, is stitched at the base to make a fan shape, and then decorated with a diamanté trim and a dramatic jewel (far right).

Fun
FLOWERS

Design Tips

Look for books on making silk or tissue-paper flowers for inspiration on different flower shapes.

Work with colors that are as close to nature as possible or go wild and use vibrant shades to make some funky, original creations.

Experiment by twisting and rolling the foam into interesting shapes—pale pink foam looks good rolled into tiny rosebuds.

Flowers are not the only shapes you can make with the foam—a black cat in profile with a jewel stone eye would look very dramatic; a more fun design think about teddy bears and clowns.

Other simple shapes that are easy to cut out include stars, hearts, butterflies, and ladybugs.

Start a collection of motif ideas. Every time a shape or idea catches your eye, try to make a tracing of it, or simply tear it out and put it into a file that's easy to refer to.

The CRAFT FOAM RUBBER USED TO MAKE THESE FUN flower pins is called neoprene and has a delightful tactile finish that fascinates adults and children alike. It is a versatile medium that is easy to obtain from craft specialists and can be used for a wide variety of projects. You can buy it in sheets, just like cardboard or felt, in an inspiring range of colors from hot brights to cool pastels. Like felt, it is easy to transfer designs to, and it cuts like a dream with scissors or a craft knife, making it possible to achieve perfect detail with more intricate shapes. It can be used not only to make simple flat designs but also is flexible enough to be rolled, twisted, and curved into more interesting three-dimensional shapes. You can also buy the foam in craft packs of pre-cut shapes like the flowers, hearts, and circles used to make this project. Pinching the edge of a circle produces a simple petal shape, which then inspired the design for this fun pin.

You Will Need

5 large yellow craft foam circles
1 small yellow craft foam circle
All-purpose, clear-drying glue
Clothespin
Pin back
Small black bead

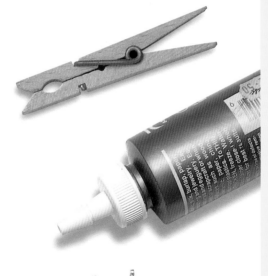

Getting Started

For this pin, make sure that the larger precut circles are 1⅛ inches / 3 cm in diameter and that the smaller circle is ¾ inch / 2 cm in diameter. Once all the petals have been glued to the center, use a pair of tweezers to position and glue the central bead.

FUN FLOWERS

1.

Put a small blob of glue on each of the larger foam circles, close to the edge. Pinch the foam at the glued point to create a petal shape.

2.

Use a clothespin to hold the shape as the glue dries.

3.

Cover the smaller circle with glue and arrange the petals in a flower shape on top. Let dry completely.

4.

Glue a pin back in position.

5.

Finish the flower by gluing a small black bead to the center point, between the petals.

Variations on a Theme

PURPLE PASSION FLOWER

Cut out carefully with scissors or a craft knife.

1. Draw or trace 5 petal shapes onto craft rubber.

2.

3. Apply glue to a contrasting-colored circle of foam and position the petals on top in the shape of a flower. Glue another circle of foam over the center and, when dry, complete with a pin back.

This black-eyed Susan is just one of the hundreds of ideas you can use craft rubber for (right).

Fantasy FISH

Design Tips

Sketch out your design ideas on paper and work out the scale and balance.

You can make a paste from a little air-dry clay mixed with water and brush it over the surface to fill in any cracks and create a smooth finish.

File rough edges with an emery board.

Like polymer clays, air-dry clays are easy to shape using the variety of cookie cutters available.

Children's arts and crafts books are a great resource for simple, stylized motifs that you can decorate with clever paint techniques and stylish color combinations.

Speed up drying time by placing the clay shape in a low-temperature oven. Experiment with test pieces of clay to find the right time and temperature.

THE DESIGN FOR THIS STYLIZED fish was inspired by the motif on a set of contemporary plates seen in a store. It was easy to re-create as a fun pin using air-dry clay as the base and adding the decorative details with special porcelain paints to make it look as if it was made of fine china. Keeping to a classic blue and white color combination added to the effect, but it would also look great painted in the bold, bright colors of exotic tropical fish. Modern air-dry clays produce a wonderful ceramic finish without the need for an expensive kiln and can be painted with acrylics, cold enamel, and ceramic paints as well as the porcelain paints used here. The clay is easy to mold, sculpt, and cut just like polymer clay and can be substituted for most of the projects that don't rely on the polymer clay colors.

You Will Need

Cardboard
Pencil
Ruler
Air-dry clay
Rolling pin
Craft knife
Emery board
White, light blue, and dark blue porcelain paints
Paintbrush
All-purpose, clear-drying glue
Pin back

Getting Started

To fill in cracks and even out rough surfaces in the clay, mix a little clay with water to form a smooth paste.

FANTASY FISH

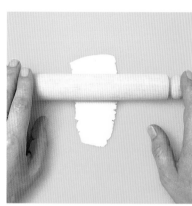

Roll out the clay to a depth of approximately ¼ inch / 0.5 cm.

Draw a template on the cardboard. To obtain the ellipse shape, use a ruler to draw a line the length of the finished pin—approximately 2½ inches / 6.5 cm. Mark the center point and 2 additional points ½ inch / 1 cm to each side. Draw a curved line from one end of the line up to the marked point and back to the other end of the line. Repeat on the other side and cut out the shape.

Place the cardboard template on top of the clay and use a craft knife to cut around it carefully. Smooth edges and any obvious cracks and let dry until completely hard. Use an emery board to file any remaining rough edges.

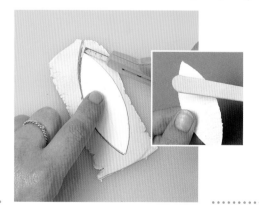

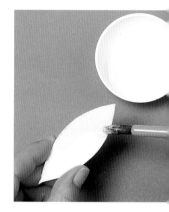

Apply a smooth paste to the clay with your fingers to fill any fine cracks and surface dents. Let dry completely.

5.

Paint both sides and edges of the shape white. Let dry (read paint instructions for drying time—the paint might still be tacky to the touch even when it appears dry).

6.

Lightly outline your design in pencil.

7.

Use blue paints to complete the design, let them dry, and then fire in the oven following the clay package instructions. Glue a pin back in place to complete.

Variations on a Theme

A star-shaped cookie cutter and vivid acrylic paints were used to create this dazzling pin (right).

A tiny circular cookie cutter was used to create this mini plate pin. Simple brush strokes used for the flower petals add to the feel of hand-painted pottery (far right).

169

Stick Pins & Hat PINS

Some of the first stick pins were those worn by people in ancient civilizations to hold their clothes together before sewing or buttons were invented. Elaborate beaded pins were frequently worn, and the more powerful the person, the more ornate were the designs. Today hat and lapel pins are largely decorative and are a great way of adding your own personal stamp to an outfit.

Hat pins can be used to totally transform a simple hat into a glamorous, expensive-looking hat, especially if it's decorated with fabulous feather plumes or an ornate collection of beads. These pins don't have to be confined to hats—they look wonderful worn on a lapel and are a perfect way to add a touch of style to a plain outfit. Shorter versions look striking as scarf pins. Pins are available with protective caps for the pointed tips from jewelry and craft suppliers and come in a variety of lengths to suit different needs. Some come with flat discs at the top, which you can decorate with all kinds of materials from traditional beads and jewel stones to jeweler's wire, feathers, and modeling clay. Feathers can be bought in every color imaginable and even dyed to match a special outfit. Natural feathers like peacock and pheasant are appealing on felt hats in muted country colors. They can be attached to the top of pins with matching thread or inserted into comple-mentary beads or even shank-backed buttons. Jeweler's wire in thicker gauges can be shaped into coils and decorated with beads or jewel stones for a totally modern look, and model-ing clay helps re-create ideas inspired by the past.

Beaded Metal
SWIRLS

Choose a pin to suit the use of the design—lapel pins are shorter than hat pins.

Experiment by bending jeweler's wire around different shapes to create a variety of designs.

The wire can also be hammered into shape to create a completely different effect—use thicker wires and a rawhide hammer or an ordinary hammer covered with a piece of suede or felt.

Look for unusual feathers—perhaps from an unused feather duster.

Beads with large holes can be slipped on after the wire has been shaped and glued to secure, or you can try beading the wire first and then carefully shaping it for a more ornate finish.

TOGETHER WITH BEADS, JEWELER'S WIRE RATES AS one of the most essential and versatile materials to have in your craft jewelry box. It comes in a variety of thicknesses and colors—real gold, silver, and copper, plus plated alternatives that are less expensive. The wire can be used to make your own basic findings or for more decorative work like these contemporary pins. The metal is soft enough to be shaped into intricate designs using a variety of objects as basic forms, from pliers to pieces of wood. The finished piece can then be attached to a purchased stick pin or to one made from the same metal and filed to a point at one end. Decorated with jewels or beads, the finished pins can be designed to coordinate with a favorite hat or outfit.

You Will Need

Jeweler's wire
Wire cutters
Needle-nosed pliers
Several beads with large center holes
All-purpose, clear-drying glue
Stick pin with protective cap

Getting Started

This piece requires jeweler's wire, about 0.05 inch / 1.2 mm thick for the metal swirls, and 0.03 inch / 0.8 mm thick for binding the metal swirls to the stick pin.

BEADED METAL SWIRLS

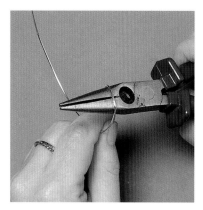

Cut 2 pieces of thick wire, each 10 inches / 25.5 cm long, and grip one end with the widest end of the pliers.

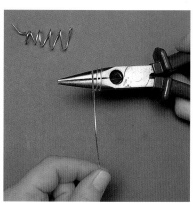

Wrap the wire around the pliers 5 or 6 times, working toward the tip. Trim the wire, leaving a short tail, and slip the coil off the pliers. Repeat for the other piece.

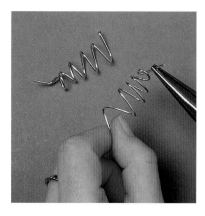

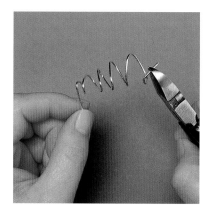

Holding the widest end of the coil with your fingers and the other end with the pliers, gently stretch out the coil. Straighten the tail at the narrowest point with pliers.

Trim the end of the first wrap to approximately ¼ inch / 0.5 cm.

5.

Place the top of the stick pin between the 2 tails left at the narrower ends of the coils and bind them together tightly with fine wire. Wrap the wire evenly and trim when the joint feels totally secure.

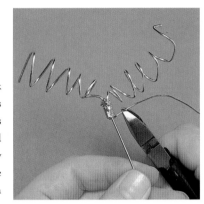

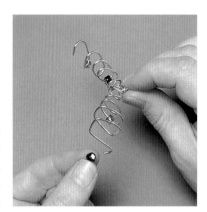

6.

Straighten out the tips at the other end enough to slip on the beads. Add as many beads as you want, slipping them over the coils toward the center but leaving them spaced out. Fold the tips of the wire back on themselves to form hooks and glue the beads securely.

7.

The beads in the center can be glued or left loose for an interesting effect.

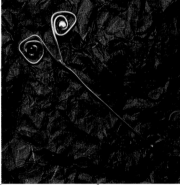

Variations on a Theme

This single coil was shaped over a wooden dowel, decorated with pearls and black beads, joined to a disc-topped lapel pin, and then decorated with a coordinating flat-backed jewel stone (right).

Here copper wire has been worked into flat spirals and the centers decorated with jewel stones (far right). Try making your own pin from wire cut and shaped to a point.

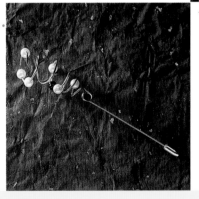

Jazzy Jeweled
PIN

THE BASE FOR THIS FUN ABSTRACT PIN WAS MADE BY layering pasted strips of newspaper over a shape cut from thick cardboard. It shows how versatile the craft of papier-mâché is; by working with very narrow strips of paper, you can cover the most intricate shapes to give them a strong, sturdy finish. In the past, craftspeople used these techniques to make tables and chairs, and in Scandinavia an entire church was built from papier-mâché! Traditionally the paper is carefully placed in even layers to create a smooth finished surface, but interesting textured finishes can be achieved by layering the paper more randomly. This then provides the perfect base for decorative paint and allows you to let your imagination run free with ideas for different finished effects. For detailed directions on making perfect papier-mâché, refer to the Golden Celtic Shield project.

You Will Need

Cardboard
Pencil
Scissors
Wallpaper paste
Paste brush
Small strips of torn newspaper
PVA glue
Gesso
Paintbrush
Gold metallic Plaka paint
Small block of plasticine
Several colorful flat-backed jewel stones
Tweezers
All-purpose, clear-drying glue
Stick pin with disc top and protective cap

Getting Started

This simple papier-mâché project involves pasting small strips of newspaper over a cardboard shape that is then painted with gesso and acrylic paint. Follow the package instructions to make a small amount of wallpaper paste.

JAZZY JEWELED PIN

1.

Draw your shape on thick cardboard freehand or with tracing paper. Cut it out carefully using sharp scissors.

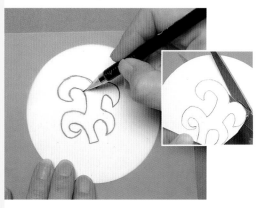

2.

Apply paste to a strip of newspaper and place it on one side of the shape so that a little extends beyond the edge. Smooth it flat with your fingers.

3.

Smooth the protruding end over to the opposite side, making sure the edge is smooth. Continue layering pasted strips over the shape, covering both sides and the edges. You will need 4 to 6 layers in all to create a firm, finished piece, and the last 2 or 3 should be painted with PVA glue instead of paste to give a more durable finish. Let dry completely.

4.

Paint with artist's gesso. This acts as an undercoat and prevents the newsprint from showing through the painted finish.

5.

Glue the pin in place at the base of the shape—this gives you something to hold when painting.

6.

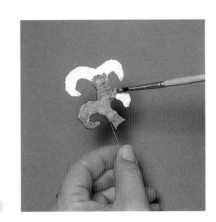

Paint both sides and the edges of the shape gold. Let dry and add another coat if necessary.

7.

Insert the point of the pin onto a block of plasticine to hold it flat and then cover it with jewel stones placed at random but highlighting the shape of the finished design.

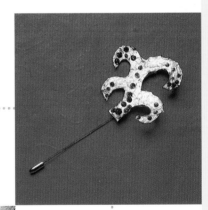

Variations on a Theme

The same shape has been painted in rich purple; textured glitter paints add a decorative finish instead of jewel stones (right).

Liquid beads are another way of adding a decorative finish. They can be used to create an abstract pattern of their own or placed in a more regular design (far right).

Marble & Pearl
PIN

Design Tips

To get the best finish from polymer modeling clays, knead well to soften and remove any air bubbles. This should then create a smooth surface when the clay is rolled out.

Leaving the clay wrapped in a plastic bag on top of a towel on a warm radiator helps speed up the softening time, especially on old clay. Alternatively, you can buy special preparations produced by the manufacturer that do the same job.

Practice getting the perfect marbled effect by working with small pieces of clay before beginning the actual project.

When you've mastered the technique of marbling, you can move on to experiment with more extensive color combinations.

Books on the history of jewelry and the styles of different periods can provide great inspiration for different shapes.

THE INSPIRATION FOR THIS UNUSUAL PIN DESIGN COMES from the strong shapes that were fashionable during the Art Deco period. The design idea is then reworked in malleable polymer clay that comes in a wide range of colors and looks wonderful blended together to create dramatic marbled effects. You can use any color combination you like to create marbled effects—with practice it is even possible to create a blend that mimics real precious stones such as lapis lazuli or malachite. The blended clay can be rolled out like pastry dough and cut into shapes with cookie cutters or a cardboard template and craft knife. Two different shapes gently pressed together will fuse when fired in a low-temperature oven. By attaching a finding to the soft clay, you can also hang charm drops for additional decoration.

You Will Need

Polymer clay in 2 colors
Rolling pin
Circular cookie cutters
or cardboard templates
Craft knife
Ruler
4 eye pins
Wire cutters
All-purpose, clear-drying glue
Varnish
2 jump rings
2 pearl drop beads
Pliers
Stick pin with disc top
and protective cap

Getting Started

Knead the Fimo with your thumbs and fingers until soft and pliable—this will prevent cracks and make it much easier to roll. Wash your hands when changing colors to prevent one color from mixing into another and spoiling the finished effect. Use 2 different cookie cutters or cardboard templates, 2 inches / 5 cm and 1 inch / 2.5 cm in diameter, to create the circular discs.

MARBLE & PEARL PIN

Roll the clay out like pastry dough to a depth of approximately ¼ inch / 0.5 cm.

Roll out a log of Fimo in each color. Wrap these around one another and roll to form a single log. Fold this in half, twist the 2 halves together, and knead to blend the colors. Continue twisting and kneading until you have the desired marbled effect.

Cut out a circle of marbled clay 1 inch / 2.5 cm in diameter, using the smaller cutter.

Select one of the colors used for marbling and roll out as before. Cut out a circle with the larger cutter and then position the smaller cutter on top, close to one edge. Cut out the smaller circle and discard. Using a ruler and craft knife, trim the shape as shown.

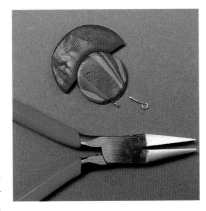

5.

Butt this crescent shape up against the marbled circle and gently smooth the joining edges. Trim 2 eye pins to about ⅜ inch / 1 cm and insert into the clay as shown. Fire in a low-temperature oven following package instructions.

6.

Add a dab of glue to secure the eye pins inserted in the clay. Varnish it to bring out the colors in the clay. Slip the pearl drops onto the eye pins, trim the wire to within ⅜ inch / 1 cm of the bead top, and make a loop with the pliers. Slip open jump rings through the loops of the beaded pins and the pins in the clay. Close to secure.

7.

Glue a stick pin in place to complete the design.

Variations on a Theme

The same idea has been adapted in plain clays to create a different shape. This time the design is finished with a central jewel stone and a coordinating glass bead drop (right).

Place several crescents of clay side by side in alternating colors and finish with a small circle of clay for another variation on the same theme (far right).

183

Links, Drops, & Bar PINS

By linking charm drops or using unusual materials you can create much more elaborate pins than the traditional stick or badge styles. These styles can be fixed to any pin finding and fastened to a coat, blouse, scarf, or hat. Look for different materials—such as pretty ribbons, wire mesh, and even shells—to create totally original designs.

Modeling clay can be shaped with cookie cutters and given textured finishes using all kinds of different objects, or it can be cut into more definite forms like starfish and decorated with pretty shell dangles. Wire mesh is pliable enough to be worked into simple or complex shapes and can be decorated with dazzling jewel stones or "found" objects such as charms from broken necklaces or bracelets. Make pretty fabrics rigid by using fabric stiffening products or simple PVA glue. This gives the fabric form and allows you to create permanent pleats and gathers. Special perforated findings can be bought with claws to clamp over corresponding pin backs, and these can be embroidered with small beads and even buttons. Pierced backs are also perfect for sewing fabric pins to because they are often difficult to join successfully to flat surfaces. Pin backs like these, together with plain metal discs and ovals, are available from jewelry, bead, and craft suppliers.

Jeweled Lace
ROSETTE

Design Tips

Experiment with different types of
fabric—ribbons are ideal, since their
edges are already neatened, but you
can also use strips of any fabric.

Apply the PVA to a scrap piece
of fabric first to see how many
coats will be required to get the
rigidity you desire.

PVA gives some fabrics an obvious
shine. Do a test piece to make sure
you are happy with the finish.

Experiment with different pin shapes
by pleating or folding the fabric
origami-style rather than just using
a plain circle.

You can also achieve different effects
by first painting or embroidering the
fabric. The colors of some embroidery
threads can run, so first paint a
small piece with PVA to test it.

T HE USE OF FABRIC IN JEWELRY DESIGN IS BECOMING increasingly popular and offers limitless opportunities for innovative ideas. Nothing is impossible when creating this kind of "soft" jewelry—let your imagination run wild. Even traditional crafts such as embroidery, quilting, and patchwork can be applied to jewelry designs. Stiffening fabric with PVA glue gives it another dimension, as this rosette pin illustrates. It is made from a length of pretty lace edging that has been gathered at one edge to create the rosette effect and then painted with PVA. The PVA gives the fabric a clear, nearly invisible, plastic-like coating that helps keep it rigid and in shape. (You can also buy prepared solutions for stiffening fabrics from craft suppliers.) Lace comes with ready-made holes that are perfect for linking charms, and the stiffened finish will prevent it from tearing. The pretty drop for this pin was taken from a broken earring, but you could easily make your own.

Getting Started

Look for lace edging with a repeating floral or figure design that is approximately 1 inch / 2.5 cm wide. Rummage around your bead or sewing box for colored glass beads, a single bead drop from a broken earring, and a single pearl bead (for the center).

Strip of lace edging
Scissors
Matching heavy thread
Needle
PVA glue
Paintbrush
A bead drop from a broken earring
or 2 pearl drop beads
and 2 colored glass beads
Pearl bead for the center
Jump ring
Pliers
Pin back

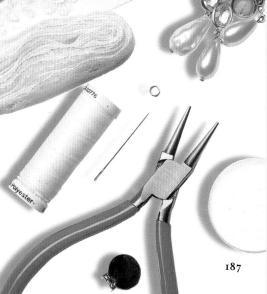

JEWELED LACE ROSETTE

1.

Cut a strip of lace
10 inches / 25.5 cm
long.

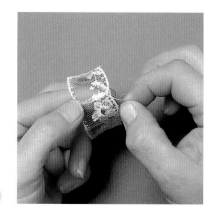

2.

Fold under the cut edge
of one of the short ends
of the lace and press
with a cool iron. Layer
this end over the other
short end to form a
circle. Slip-stitch to
hold in place.

3.

Make a knot in one
end of a piece of thread.
Sew a row of long
running stitches along
the bottom edge of the
lace circle.

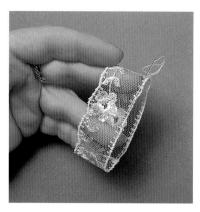

4.

Pull the thread up so
that the lace forms a
rosette shape.

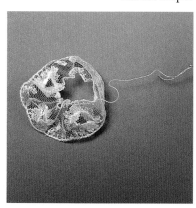

5.

With the needle still threaded, stitch through the center of the gathered lace to secure.

6.

Carefully paint the rosette with a light coat of PVA glue and let dry. Add another coat if required.

7.

To finish, glue or sew a pearl to the center point of the rosette. Slip a jump ring through the lace near one edge and then add the bead charm, closing the jump ring to secure. Sew or glue to a pin back.

Variations on a Theme

Here the same idea has been worked with a pretty chiffon ribbon. This time the fabric has been stiffened with hairspray to make a pin in an instant and, since the fabric is too fine to add a drop to, a dramatic jewel stone adds decorative interest at the center (right).

A finely pleated ribbon rosette makes a sensational pin that could be worn on a lapel or used to decorate a hat (far right).

Textured
EFFECTS

Experiment with different textures—mixing several together can create special effects, especially if worked like a patchwork or sampler on a small area.

String arranged in a shape and glued on cardboard can be pressed into the clay, as can high-relief rubber stamps.

For a natural theme, you could use tree bark, pieces of wood, leaves, or shells.

Toothpicks or wooden skewers can be used to draw stylized or abstract patterns in the clay.

For an alternative to indented patterns, use extra pieces of clay in the same or contrasting colors to form a raised texture.

To highlight your design, use a fine paintbrush to paint deep grooves or raised patterns on the clay.

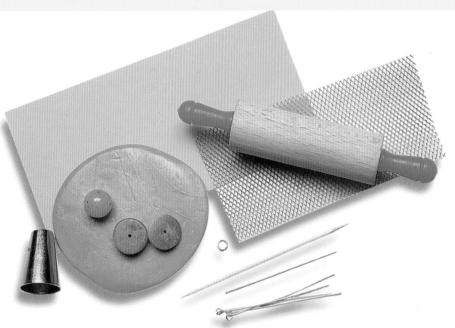

PERFECTLY SMOOTH, even surfaces are ideal for painting and decorating in all manners, but you can also have fun adding texture. This is simple to do on synthetic clays before they are fired, because the surface is receptive to anything pressed onto it. You can use an endless variety of objects—this project and the variations shown used a piece of wire mesh, a nutmeg grater, and a shell. You could also try a cheese grater, string, coins—anything that has an interesting textured finish. Textural effects can also be achieved by adding relief details using additional clay in the same color or in contrasting colors. Small pieces of clay are easy to add to the surface and will fuse when fired in a low-temperature oven.

Getting Started

To gauge how much pressure is needed to get a clean, textured finish, practice pressing the wire mesh or sieve into spare pieces of clay.

You Will Need

Block of polymer clay
Cardboard
Pencil
Compass
Rolling pin
Craft knife
Top of a piping bag or similar round "cutter"
Toothpick
Wire mesh (or metal sieve)
Several beads to coordinate with color of clay
4 eye pins
Straight pin
Wire cutters
Jump ring
Pliers
Pin back
All-purpose, clear-drying glue

TEXTURED EFFECTS

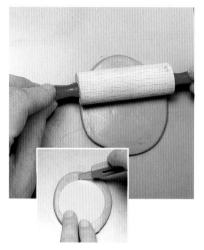

2. Use the top from a piping bag to cut out a central circle, forming a doughnut-like shape.

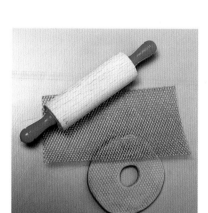

1. Knead the clay until warm and pliable, then roll out like pastry dough on a flat surface to a depth of about ⅜ inch / 1 cm. Draw a circle, 3 inches / 7.5 cm in diameter, on a piece of cardboard and cut it out. Place the circle on the clay and cut it out carefully with a craft knife.

3. Pierce a hole from the outside edge to the center with a toothpick.

4. Place the piece of wire mesh or a kitchen sieve over the surface of the doughnut and press down firmly (use the rolling pin if working with mesh).

5.

Use the toothpick to draw lines in the clay that radiate out from the center. Then fire in a low-temperature oven following clay package instructions.

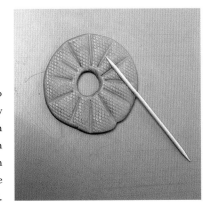

6.

Using pliers, make a spiral from an eye pin working up the wire from the opposite end to the eye.

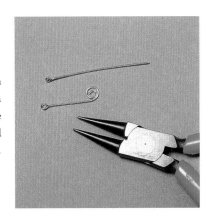

7.

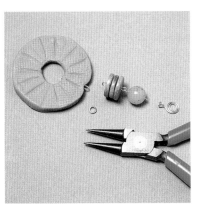

Push a head pin through the hole already made in the pin base, inserting it from the center of the doughnut shape. Turn a loop in the protruding end. Make the charm drop by linking together a group of beads and a single bead wired with eye pins. Add the metal spiral to the last bead, and join the charm to the loop on the pin base using a jump ring. Finish by gluing a pin back to the wrong side.

Variations on a Theme

For this pin, texture has been added by pressing a metal nutmeg grater into the surface (right).

This pin looks like a piece of ancient sculpture, but the design was created by pressing a shell into stone-imitation polymer clay (far right).

Pop-Art
PIN

Design Tips

Experiment with the variety of different-shaped punches available —look for hearts, teddy bears, birds, butterflies, and more from craft specialists.

Artist's mat board is perfect for making brooch bases. Try cutting out different shapes—ovals, oblongs, hearts, flowers, circles, and triangles are easy, but you could also experiment with more abstract shapes.

If you can't find neoprene, sequins are a great substitute and can be used to create more glamorous finished pieces.

Tiny flat-backed jewel stones can also be used to create dazzling effects.

Paint the cardboard different colors to vary the background or buy colored mount board.

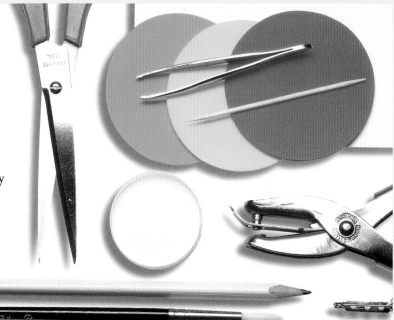

N EOPRENE IS AN EXCITING ADDITION to the wide range of craft materials currently available. It has a wonderfully tactile finish that is like soft rubber and fascinates adults and children alike. It is extremely versatile and can be used to create flat motifs as well as three-dimensional shapes—it can even be used to make chunky, rolled beads in the same way as paper. Available from craft specialists in sheet form or pre-cut shapes like flowers, hearts, and circles, it comes in a wide range of colors. You can draw shapes on it easily and cut out intricate details with scissors or a craft knife. For this design, a single hole punch was used to cut out tiny circles, which were then glued to a cardboard base in a pattern and colors inspired by Pop Art designs of the 1960s.

Getting Started

Tweezers are useful for picking up the tiny neoprene circles, which should be placed so that they just touch each other. A toothpick will help you position the circles exactly.

You Will Need

Neoprene in 3 different colors (red, orange, and yellow suit the theme)
Ruler
Pencil
Small piece of mat board or thick cardboard
Craft knife or scissors
Single-hole punch
All-purpose, clear-drying glue
Tweezers
Toothpick
Acrylic paint
Paintbrush
Pin back

POP-ART PIN

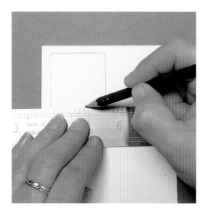

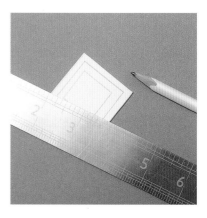

Draw the pattern on the cardboard square to use as a guideline when gluing the circles in place.

Draw a square, 1¾ inches / 4.5 cm, on the mat board and cut it out using a craft knife or sharp scissors.

Use the hole punch to cut out tiny circles from each of the different-colored pieces of neoprene—approximately 30 red, 20 orange, and 16 yellow.

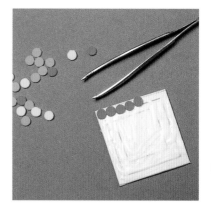

Apply glue to the surface of the cardboard and start the first horizontal line of circles.

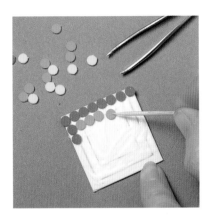

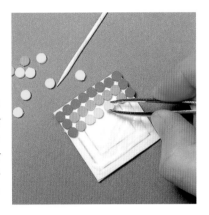

5.

Start the vertical line to
help set the pattern,
then add the next color.

6.

Glue the rest of the
circles in place, working
in lines from top to
bottom and adding
more glue if it begins
to dry out.

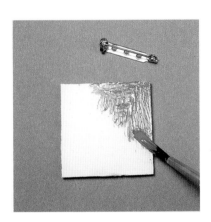

7.

Paint the back and
sides of the square in
a coordinating color.
When the paint is dry,
complete the design
by gluing a pin back
in position.

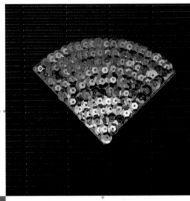

Variations on a Theme

Tiny beads in jazzy colors glued to a simple base shape create a dazzling pin (right).

A pretty fan shape has been created by cutting out a rounded triangle from mat board
and covering with sequins in several shades of the same color (far right).

Clips & COMBS

For centuries, women have been using ornamental decorations to secure their hair in the latest style. Two of the most popular and practical designs today are the clip-fastening slide and the basic comb, which come in a wide variety of forms and can be used to hold anything from a ponytail to a chignon in place.

Clips and combs can be as simple or as ornate as you choose and are one of the simplest pieces of jewelry to make. You can buy metal clip-fastening bases from craft stores to make your own unique designs from papier-mâché or polymer clays or, alternatively, dress up plain plastic combs and slides with jewel stones, satin ribbons, or pretty silk flowers. Dazzling cut-glass stones set in mounts look sensational simply glued to plain metal clip bases, or you can create more interesting effects by anchoring strings of pretty beads to preformed holes in the base—twist, weave, or braid several strings together to achieve really dramatic finishes.

Today's realistic-looking silk flowers are ideal for turning a simple clip or comb into something more special.

All the designs that follow are very versatile; once you have mastered the techniques shown, you might be inspired to interpret the basic idea in different ways. By adjusting the shape, color combinations, and decorative details, you can create many different effects.

Dazzling glass stones produce the best faux jewel effects. They can be found in a wide variety of shapes, including hearts and flowers.

Less-expensive acrylic and plastic jewel stones are also available in a fabulous range of colors and shapes.

Use the preformed holes on basic barrette clips to attach ornately beaded strings and try braiding, weaving, and twisting several together to create different effects.

Look for striking beads to use to decorate plain barrette clips—beads with flat surfaces can be glued directly to the clip's metal base, but round beads need to be wired or strung onto thread.

Dazzling
DIAMONDS

ACCORDING TO THE OLD SONG, DIAMONDS ARE A girl's best friend, and if you can't afford the real thing, sparkling cut glass has the same dazzling effect from a distance. The faceted jewel stones used to make this project come in faux emerald, sapphire, and a multitude of other precious jewel finishes. The settings can be bought with holes ready for sewing and threading, or plain for soldering, and both can be glued to basic barrettes to make unique, expensive-looking hair accessories. The basic idea invites experimentation; a collection of beautiful ceramic beads in patterns inspired by ancient Far Eastern dynasties looks superb simply glued in place. For another sparkling alternative, anchor strings of boldly colored glass rocailles to preformed holes in metal slide bases and braid, weave, or twist them to create different effects.

You Will Need

Cardboard
Epoxy adhesive
Spatula
Tweezers
Faceted jewel stones and matching mounts
Barrette base
Needle-nosed pliers

Getting Started

Look for a base that suits the thickness of your hair and that holds your hair in place for your chosen style. Measure the length of the base to gauge how many jewels you will need.

DAZZLING DIAMONDS

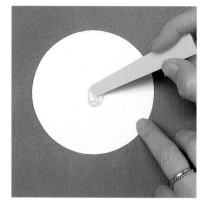

Squeeze the epoxy onto a piece of cardboard. Mix the two elements together thoroughly with a spatula, following the package instructions.

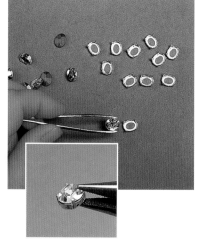

Using tweezers, carefully place each stone in a mount and make sure it is level. Use the tips of a pair of needle-nosed pliers to fold the claws of the mount over the stones to secure them.

Make sure the metal barrette is clean and grease-free before applying a layer of epoxy.

Dab a small amount of epoxy onto the back of each mount and place it on the clip. Add as many stones as needed to completely cover the barrette base.

Variations on a Theme

BLUE NOTES BARRETTE

1.

Cut three lengths
of tiger tail. Slip one
end of each through
the hole at one end of
the clip and secure with
a calotte crimp—this
gives a neater finish
than knots.

2.

Thread beads on each
of the outside threads
and attach to the
opposite end of the
barrette with a calotte
crimp as in step 1. Bead
the middle thread and
work it over and under
the others to create a
woven effect.

Just a few special beads mimicking classic china designs look sensational when glued in
place. Create designs using the same type of beads, or mix coordinating colors and vary
the way they are placed to achieve more original effects (right).

Romantic
RIBBONS

Design Tips

Keep a scrap bag of ribbon and threads left over from other projects—they are perfect for decorating objects like hair combs.

Experiment with narrow strips of fabric as well as ribbons and threads—strips of denim or chambray can be used to create a sportier look for everyday wear.

Natural or dyed raffia is an excellent alternative to ribbons or cords.

The width of your ribbon will determine the size of a finished rosette—the wider the ribbon, the larger the rosette.

Stitch rosettes of different sizes together and finish with a central bead to create a pretty ribbon "flower."

B ASIC HAIR COMBS PROVIDE THE IDEAL BASE FOR creating pretty hair accessories because they can be dressed up with a wonderful variety of materials. Narrow ribbons, colorful silk embroidery threads, or fine satin cords can all be used to transform a basic plastic comb into something exceptional, especially if decorated with pretty coordinating beads or jazzy jewel stones. Cords and threads can be twisted or braided to create different looks, and ribbons look wonderful gathered into tiny rosettes that can be strewn across the top of a comb. Richly colored velvet ribbons decorated with sparkling diamanté are a wonderful combination for evening wear, and softer-hued satin, chiffon, or organza ribbons teamed with lustrous pearls look sensational worn by a bride or her attendants.

You Will Need

All-purpose, clear-drying glue
Plain plastic hair comb
Narrow, double-sided satin ribbon
Clothespin
Scissors
10–15 rice pearls
Tweezers

Getting Started

The amount of ribbon required depends on its width and the depth of the top of the comb. To get an idea of approximately how much you need, wrap the comb with string and measure this length.

ROMANTIC RIBBONS

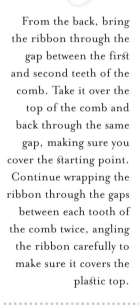

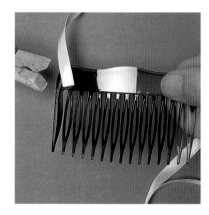

Dab a little glue on the right side of the comb, close to one end.

Place the end of the ribbon on the glue and hold it in place with a clothespin while it dries.

From the back, bring the ribbon through the gap between the first and second teeth of the comb. Take it over the top of the comb and back through the same gap, making sure you cover the starting point. Continue wrapping the ribbon through the gaps between each tooth of the comb twice, angling the ribbon carefully to make sure it covers the plastic top.

Before taking the ribbon through the last gap for the second time, dab a little glue close to the edge.

5.

Take the ribbon through to the back of the comb, trim, and secure with a dab of glue.

6.

To complete the comb, glue rice pearls to the ribbon, positioning them with tweezers to make sure they are evenly spaced.

Variations on a Theme

1.

Tiny rosettes of pastel and deep-pink ribbon look wonderful glued to cover the top of this simple comb. Cut two 2 ½-inch / 6.4-cm lengths of ribbon (¼ inch / 0.6 cm wide) in several shades of the same color. Join the short ends to form a circle and then run a gathering stitch along one long edge. Carefully pull this up and secure to form the rosettes. Glue in place on the top edge of a basic plastic hair comb.

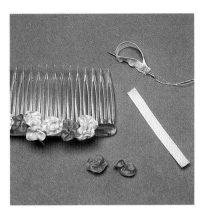

Three rosettes made from the same ribbon are grouped together to create a stylish look (right).

Floral
FANTASY

Design Tips

Choose flowers carefully. You'll create a more authentic look by opting for varieties that are actually in season and that look the most genuine.

Larger blooms look best on combs or slides that can be set to the side or back of the head rather than dead center on a headband.

Newspaper and magazine reports of designer runway shows are a great source of inspiration for designs. Many top couturiers, especially the French, decorate models' hair with elegant or witty floral creations.

Search out books that show you how to make your own silk flowers and have fun creating totally original designs.

Simple designs create the most realistic effect, and a dab of scent helps complete the feel.

Hair looks and feels wonderful dressed with fresh flowers, but, sadly, this is not always practical—real flowers don't last long and are easily damaged. With care you can create a similar effect with today's fabulous array of silk flowers—the shapes and colors look so realistic that it is almost impossible to tell the difference from a distance. The most authentic-looking silk flowers are often the most expensive, but few are needed, so it is worth spending a little extra to achieve the right feel. Simply wire or glue dramatic single blooms or pretty sprays to combs, clips, or headbands to add the perfect finishing touch to a special outfit and add a spritz of eau de cologne to complete the effect.

You Will Need

Small silk flowers and pretty leaves
Scissors
Fine florist's or jeweler's wire
All-purpose, clear-drying glue
Tweezers
Plastic hair comb
Round-nosed pliers

Getting Started

Choose a hair comb with a patterned open-work top edge, like the one shown—these are much easier to wire flowers to. Make sure the wire is bound tightly around the flowers and the comb to secure them in place.

FLORAL FANTASY

1. Cut a selection of flowers in the main color, keeping each stalk as long as possible.

2. Select a single large leaf or several small leaves; then cut two or three fully open flowers plus one or two buds in the contrast color.

5. Trim the stalks just below the base of one or two flowers in the main color and build a corsage effect by gluing them in place where required. Using tweezers, add a few buds in the contrast color in the same way.

3. Using fine wire, bind three or four flowers in the main color tightly together in an attractive group.

4. Join this spray of flowers to the leaf in the same way.

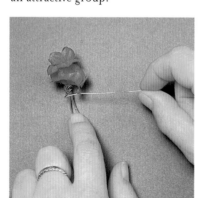

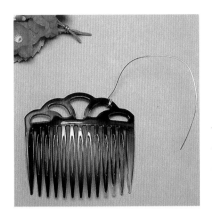

6. Wrap a length of wire tightly to the top edge of the comb approximately three-quarters of the way across.

7. Use the wire to bind the main corsage to the comb, wrapping it around the stems several times with pliers.

8. Wire together a smaller group of flowers in both the main and contrast colors; then carefully bind these to the comb to cover the spot where you joined the main corsage.

Variations on a Theme

A single bloom nestling on a bed of leaves completely disguises a very ordinary plastic hair clip (right).

A simple row of daisy heads, glued in place, transforms a functional hair comb into a desirable accessory in minutes (far right).

Beautiful BANDS

Bands in one form or another have been used to decorate and hold hair in place since the beginning of time, and the styles have varied from simple ribbons to ornate jewel-encrusted circlets and tiaras. A famous fresco from the Royal Palace at Knossos shows ladies of the Minoan court wearing ribbons just above their foreheads and tied at the nape of the neck; the rest of their hair is threaded with chains of precious jewels. Books on the history of fashion—and hairstyles in particular—illustrate wonderful examples like this and are a great source of inspiration for design ideas.

The headband has recently become fashionable again, and a simple plastic or fabric-covered headband provides the perfect base for all kinds of decorative finishes. They can be as modest or as fancy as you choose, to suit your own personal style or a particular special occasion. You can create all kinds of different effects with the amazing variety of materials available, including luxurious braids and dazzling faux jewels. Plain white plastic bases are available from craft suppliers, but you can also use the ideas shown here to dress up an inexpensive band bought at a local drugstore.

When working out your design, it is important to create an overall balanced effect. Position motifs and any decorative detail with care so that they form a regular pattern and keep their sizes in proportion.

Hot
SPOTS

Experiment with the variety of different shaped punches available—look for hearts, teddy bears, birds, butterflies, and more from craft and art stores.

Basic plastic headbands are available from a drugstore or department store. They can be painted different colors using acrylic paints, which remain flexible when dry.

The band can be painted in any color—choose one to match a favorite outfit and select neoprene colors to coordinate.

A more dramatic effect can be achieved by sewing brightly colored buttons to a padded fabric band. Use a curved craft needle to make sewing the buttons easier.

Tiny flat-backed jewel stones are another alternative that can be used to create similar, more dazzling finishes.

N EOPRENE IS A FASCINATING ADDITION TO THE WIDE
range of craft materials currently available. It has a
wonderfully tactile finish that is like soft rubber and is
extremely versatile. Use it to create flat motifs or three-dimensional shapes—it can even be used to make chunky rolled beads
in the same way as you would with paper. Available from craft
stores in sheet form or precut shapes like flowers, hearts, and
circles, neoprene comes in a wide range of colors. You can draw
shapes on it easily and cut intricate details with scissors or
a craft knife. For this fun design, a single-hole punch
was used to make tiny circles, which were then glued
to a painted plastic headband in a five-dice pattern.
A craft pack of circles in bright assorted colors is
perfect for this design, because buying individual
sheets in all the colors would be wasteful unless you
have other projects in mind.

You Will Need

Plastic headband
Emery board
Black acrylic paint
Paintbrush
Neoprene in 6 different colors
Single-hole punch
Tweezers
All-purpose, clear-drying glue

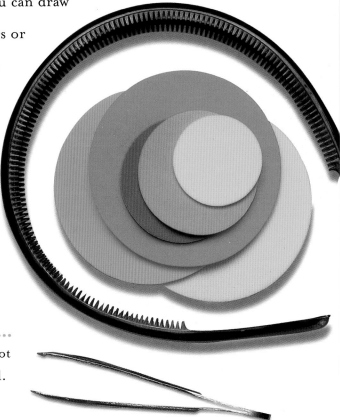

Getting Started

The five-dice pattern used for this project gives a polka-dot
effect but keeps the overall design regular and symmetrical.
By working with six colors, each pattern will be different.

HOT SPOTS

Scuff the surface of the band lightly with an emery board to provide a surface that the paint can adhere to. Don't be too rough or else scratches will show through the paint.

Use the hole punch to cut tiny circles in different colors from the neoprene—the number required will depend on how you space them.

Paint the band completely and let it dry balanced on the edge of a jar.

Using tweezers, position the circles on the painted band, alternating the colors and working in a pattern like the five on a pair of dice, and glue them in place.

Variations on a Theme

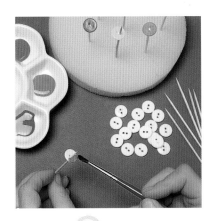

1.

A more dramatic finish can be achieved with buttons sewn to a padded fabric band. Support each button on a toothpick and paint the entire surface in a bright color. Use four or five colors to get the best effect. Place the toothpick in a piece of foam or plasticine, and let dry.

2.

Using six strands of embroidery cotton, tie a knot in one end and make a small stitch on the right side of the band close to one end. Sew on the first button, positioning it so that it covers the starter knot. Bring the needle out where the next button is to be placed—they should be evenly spaced along the band.

3.

Sew on the last button, work a couple of tiny oversew stitches under, and insert the needle back into the fabric toward the center of the band, bringing it out on a side edge as far up as you can. Pull the thread taut and cut—the tail end should disappear inside the band.

Glue flat-backed crystal stones to a thin headband for a sparkling hair accessory to wear on special occasions (right).

217

Beautiful
BRAIDS

Design Tips

You don't need a long length of braid; interesting bargain buys can be found in end-of-roll boxes.

Look for ornate braids, especially beaded ones, at antique fairs to make a really special band.

Experiment and plan your design before working on the real thing—use double-sided tape to secure in position temporarily.

Plain bands can be bought from jewelry suppliers and painted with acrylic paints to coordinate with your chosen braid.

As an alternative to braids, embroider plain fabric-covered bands with colorful threads. To add further texture and shape to the band, work the design using simple stitches threaded with beads or sequins.

W ITH A PIECE OF BRAID, a selection of beads in several shades of the same color, and a little imagination, you can transform a basic fabric band into a striking hair decoration. Braids available for dressmaking and home furnishing can be used for the ideas shown here. They can be plain, or patterned in smooth or textured finishes, and come in every color imaginable. For this project, a colorful braid was carefully beaded in coordinating colors to highlight the bold pattern and sewn with invisible thread to a plain padded band. The sparkling sequined variation was bought already beaded and is perfect for special evenings. A silky textured braid wrapped around a plain band and finished with ribbon roses could be worn by a bridesmaid for a summer wedding.

You Will Need

Padded fabric hair band
Tape measure
Length of braid (about 18 inches /
45.7 cm, depending on the band)
All-purpose, clear-drying glue
Selection of coordinating
embroidery beads
Beading needle
Thread in several shades
of the same color
Invisible thread
Scissors

Getting Started

To determine the amount of beads you will use when decorating your own braid, count the number of beads used in one inch of braid and multiply by the length of the band.

BEAUTIFUL BRAIDS

1.

Measure the band and add 1 inch / 2.5 cm to allow for two ½-inch / 1.3-cm hems.

2.

Cut the braid to the correct length.

3.

Turn ½ inch / 1.3 cm to the wrong side at each end and glue in place or hem with invisible thread.

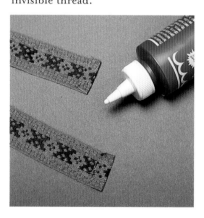

4.

Using the braid's pattern as a guide, work out where you are going to stitch the beads. For this design, beads in the two main colors of the braid were used to highlight the geometric pattern.

5.

Sew one color in place first, working clusters on the same length of thread and single beads individually. Use a tiny backstitch under each bead to hold them in position securely.

6.

Sew the second colored beads in place in the same way as the first.

7.

Oversew the braid to the band using invisible thread, taking care to keep the tension even.

Variations on a Theme

Glittering gold sequined braid was glued directly to a plain band to make this glamorous evening hair decoration (right).

Textured silky braid and pretty ribbon roses combine to make a headband that is perfect for summer weddings (far right).

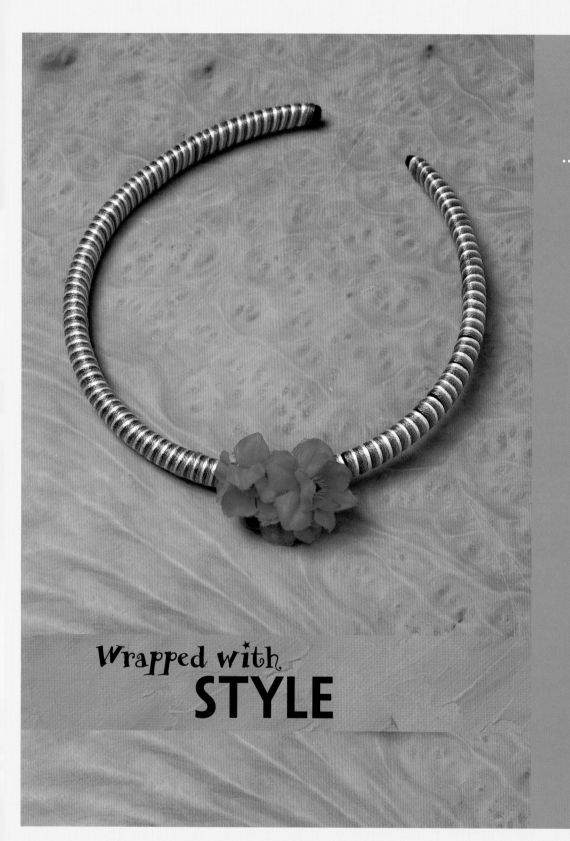

Wrapped with STYLE

A SIMPLE PLASTIC HEADBAND PROVIDES THE PERFECT foil for creative decoration and can be bought at little cost from department stores, drugstores, and craft stores. They can be decorated simply by gluing attractive beads, jewels, and shells in position or given a fancier finish by covering them completely with colorful threads or glamorous fabrics. Wrapping basic bands with strands of embroidery cottons or silks is an easy way to make a hair accessory to coordinate with a favorite outfit and takes no time at all. You can also use a variety of other materials in the same way, including pretty braids, cords, ribbons, raffia, and even decorative papers. Add a flamboyant finish with a spray of silk flowers, an ornate charm, or rich bead embroidery.

You Will Need

Basic plastic headband
Emery board
Skeins of embroidery threads
in different colors
Scissors
All-purpose, clear-drying glue
Clamp
Coordinating silk flowers

Getting Started

Measure the length of the band. Quickly wrap about one-fourth of the band, measure this length and multiply it by 4 to give you the approximate amount of thread required—remember to add a little extra for the ends.

WRAPPED WITH STYLE

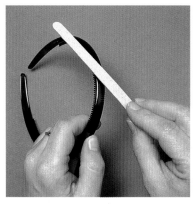

1.

Scuff the plastic band with an emery board to provide a surface for the glue to adhere to and stop the threads from sliding around.

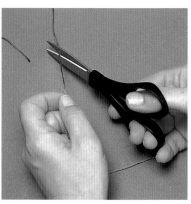

2.

Following the directions in *Getting Started*, cut threads to length. Three colors in the same shade were used to make this design.

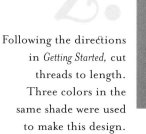

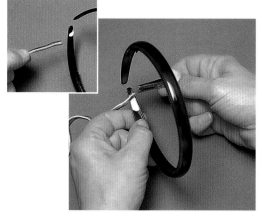

4.

Dab a small amount of glue on the inside edge of the band and place the group of threads on top. Use a clamp to hold the threads in position while the glue sets.

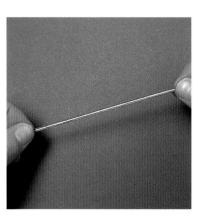

3.

Smooth the threads out so that they lie side by side.

5.

Wrap the threads tightly and evenly around the band, adding an occasional blob of glue to hold them in place.

6.

Trim the spray of flowers, cutting each stalk as closely as possible to the bloom.

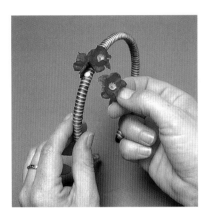

7.

Glue the flowers to the band in an attractive grouping and let dry resting on a jar or mug.

Variations on a Theme

Pleated organza and the charm from a broken earring decorate this plain padded fabric band. Sew a strip of fabric into a tube two to three times longer than the band and wide enough to cover the broadest section of the band (right).

Pretty braid and bold silk flowers were used to transform a basic band into a stunning bridal accessory (far right).

Hair SLIDES

The idea of securing hair in place with a simple pin was originally used by the ancient civilizations of Egypt, Greece, and Rome, thousands of years before clip-fastening mechanisms had been invented. Today's designs use the pin to secure both the hair and a decorative base in place and are one of the easiest styles of hair ornaments to make.

Hair slides can be any style, from chic to fun and funky. The pins are easy to make from wooden skewers, which can be cut to size and decorated in a variety of ways—paint them to match the base or wrap them with satin ribbons and fine fancy cords. Look for unusual ideas like a children's plastic embroidery needle or the cable needles used to create intricate textured knitting designs. The bases can be fashioned from an infinite variety of materials including cardboard, polymer clay, fabric, and even papier-mâché.

Once you have mastered the techniques that follow, you can create your own variations inspired by the same themes. You can also use some of the ideas for clips shown in the first section and position the holes to take the pin, where required.

Shining
STAR

Design Tips

Position the holes for the pin and curve rigid bases so that they sit neatly on your chosen hair style—the curve needed to secure a ponytail is greater than that required to hold your hair in a chignon. Use a store-bought design that fits the required style as a guide, or wrap plasticine or air-dry clay in plastic (so it won't get in your hair) and use it to make a template.

A useful source for basic motifs are catalogues illustrating stamps and stencils; for more elaborate designs, look at history books and the patterns used by ancient civilizations.

Draw your design onto tracing paper and transfer it to the metal by following the outline with a darning needle, making light indentations where you intend to position the holes, or work the design freehand using a china marker.

Use tin cutters to cut out thicker metals and wear protective gloves and glasses.

THE INSPIRATION FOR THE PIERCED
design of this hair slide comes from
traditional punched tin work
popular with the Shaker movement. It not
only is easy to master, but also provides scope for
creating a wide variety of different motifs once you gain
a little experience and get used to the feel of the metal.
Spectacular relief designs can also be worked on the metal simply
by using the tip of a knitting needle over a traced design. Once
you have mastered the basic punched-tin techniques you can experiment with more elaborate designs. For example, stars, moons,
hearts, flowers, stylized animals, or insects are easy shapes to cut
from the sheet metal. Embellish them with either pierced or etched
patterns to make original hair slides or clip-fastening barrettes.

You Will Need

Tracing paper
Thick cardboard
Steel ruler
Craft knife
Sheet metal
Darning needle
PVA glue
Scissors or tin cutters
Single-hole punch
Panel pin
Small tin hammer
All-purpose, clear-drying glue
Wooden skewer
Silver paint
Paintbrush

Getting Started

You will need a piece of sheet metal approximately 8 inches x 5 inches /
20.3 cm x 12.7 cm. Draw out the shape on paper first and place tracing
paper over it. With a pencil, transfer the motif onto the tracing paper in
dot form. Space the dots evenly and make sure the design fits centrally on
the barrette.

SHINING STAR

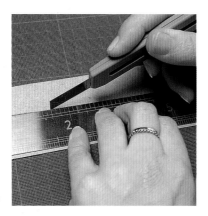

1. Cut out an oblong of cardboard 3½ inches / 8.9 cm x 1½ inches / 3.8 cm using a craft knife for smooth, even edges.

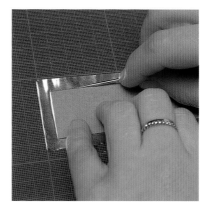

2. Center the cardboard on the piece of metal, leaving a ⅜-inch / 1-cm border on all edges. Use the tip of a darning needle to draw around the cardboard, impressing the shape in the metal. Paint both sides of the cardboard mount with PVA glue to give it flexibility. Cut out another piece of metal to the exact size of the cardboard to use as a backing.

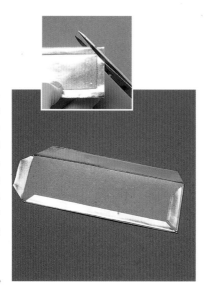

3. Use scissors or tin cutters to cut across each corner at a 45° angle. Place the PVA-coated cardboard mount back on the piece of metal and fold over all four edges along the indented lines.

4. Measure and mark the positions for the holes to hold the barrette pin on the cardboard-mounted main piece and the backing—these should be ¼ inch / 0.6 cm in from the edge and positioned centrally across the width. Punch out holes using a hole punch.

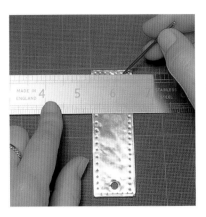

5.

Using a steel ruler as a guide, mark the border pattern with the tip of the needle, making small indentations in the metal. Try to place the marks at regular intervals.

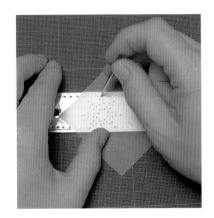

6.

Position the tracing of the motif centrally on the metal and transfer by pressing the tip of the needle through each pencil dot. Place the shape on a suitable surface and gently hammer a panel pin through each indentation on both the border and the motif to give the design greater definition.

7.

Glue the backing in place using an all-purpose glue, taking care not to get any on the front of the barrette. Let dry. Trim a wooden skewer to size and paint it silver. Gently curve the barrette around a mug and insert the pin.

Variations on a Theme

This stunning copper design was inspired by the decoration on an ancient Celtic shield. The intricate pattern was traced onto the soft metal with a knitting needle (right).

The background of a Phoenician stone relief inspired this ornate pattern (far right), which was drawn on soft-sheet aluminum in the same way as the copper Celtic shield.

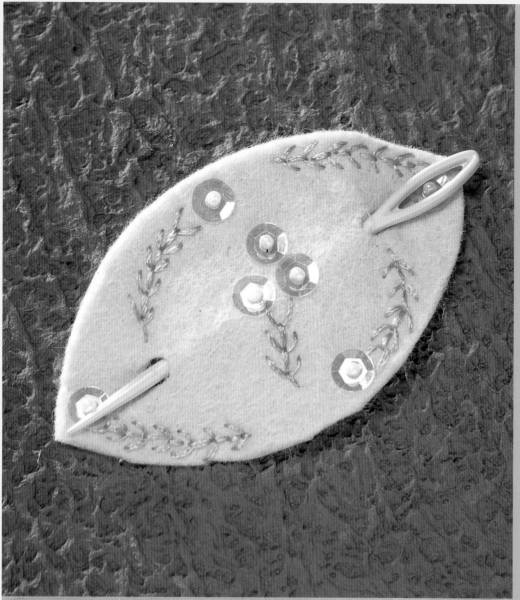

Enchanting
EMBROIDERED FELT

T HE USE OF FABRIC IN jewelry design has added another dimension to the craft and opened up a whole new world of design ideas. If you can use a needle and thread, you can transform remnants of fabric, scraps of embroidery thread, and leftover beads into pretty barrettes. Simple embroidery stitches worked by hand or on the sewing machine add texture and detail to simple fabric shapes—choose several subtle shades of the same color for a dainty finish or bold, bright metallics for something more flamboyant. Complementary beads and sequins can be used as delicate highlights or in greater numbers to create a rich, ornate finished look. Transforming your finished design into a barrette is easy with the wide range of iron-on adhesives available—they fuse the fabric to cardboard, leather, and even wood.

You Will Need

Cardboard
Compass
Pencil
Scissors
Felt (a 5-inch / 12.7-cm square)
Piece of firm iron-on interfacing
Embroidery silk
Embroidery needle
Sequins
Tiny embroidery pearl beads
Single-hole punch
Plastic needle to fasten the barrette
Iron-on adhesive

Getting Started

To draw an oval, first draw a circle 2 inches / 5.1 cm in diameter. With the compass set to the same measurement, move the point to the edge of the circle and draw an arc, taking the pencil from edge to edge, passing across the center point of the drawn circle.

ENCHANTING EMBROIDERED FELT

1. Draw an oval on the cardboard as described in *Getting Started* and cut it out. Place the interfacing on the felt and cut to size, then iron on following the instructions provided.

2. Place the cardboard template on top of the interfacing, trace it in pencil, and cut it out.

3. Mark the position of your chosen motifs on the interfacing. Using two strands of silk, embroider the design— this design is worked in a pretty feather stitch.

4. Add sequins as required. Working with a single strand of silk, bring the needle through the central hole of the sequin from the wrong side. Take the needle through a tiny pearl bead and back through the central hole of the sequin. Tie off on the wrong side.

5. Measure and mark the positions for the barrette-pin holes and cut out using a hole punch. The holes should be placed in line with the points of the oval and approximately ¾ inch / 1.9 cm in from the edges, depending on the size of the fastening pin.

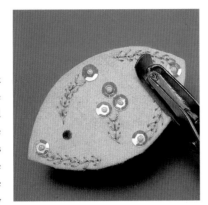

6. Check the length of the fastening pin and set the holes appropriately so it sits centrally on the motif as shown.

7.

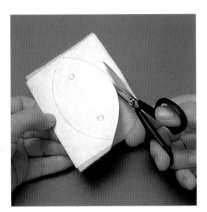

Cut another oval from the remaining felt and apply iron-on adhesive to one side following the instructions. Remove the paper backing and place the embroidered motif right-side down on top of a towel. Place the adhesive side of the second oval on top, matching edges exactly and press following the instructions provided.

Variations on a Theme

This safari design fabric was decorated with tiny beads and textured glitter paints. Back with suede or leather and punch out holes for the pin (right).

Embroider a paisley shape with tiny beads to highlight the colors and pattern and back with suede, leather, or felt. To make the pin, wrap a wooden skewer with twisted paper cord (far right).

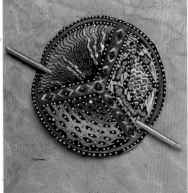

Mock Croc
BARRETTE

THIS FUN CROCODILE HAIR SLIDE is just one of many creations you can make using today's versatile polymer modeling clays. They come in a wide range of colors that can be used to make plain shapes, like the crocodile, or multicolored designs like the fish and butterfly variations. Once kneaded, the clay can be rolled out like just like pastry and cut using a cardboard template and craft knife or preformed cookie cutters. The surface is soft enough to add texture and design detail in other colors. The finished shape needs to sit on something curved as it is baked to create the right shape for a barrette, and you may need to experiment a little to get it just right.

You Will Need

Cardboard
Pencil
Scissors
Block of green polymer clay
Rolling pin
Craft knife
Wooden skewer or toothpick
Varnish
Paintbrush
Copper wire
Round-nosed pliers
Verdigris-copper beads
Flat-backed emerald crystals
All-purpose, clear-drying glue

Getting Started

To ensure that the hair slide will have a perfect fit, wrap a strip of plasticine approximately the same length and width as the finished design in clear plastic wrap and position it on your head. Insert a wooden skewer through both holes, then carefully remove it, keeping the shape. Use this as a pattern for the clay shape and bake the finished design over something oven-proof with a similar curve.

237

MOCK CROC BARRETTE

Break off half the block
of clay and knead until
pliable. Roll out on a
flat surface to a depth of
approximately ¼ inch /
0.6 cm.

1.

Draw your motif
on cardboard and
cut it out.

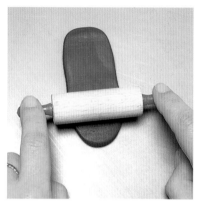

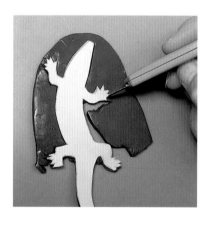

3.

Place the cardboard
template on top of
the rolled-out clay.
Carefully cut around
the outline of the
shape using the tip of
the craft knife.

4.

Clean up any ragged
edges and go over
details like the toes to
get a perfect shape.
(The edges of the
clay can be smoothed
with an emery board
after baking.)

5.

Use the tip of a wooden skewer to texture the clay to look like crocodile skin and make indentations for the eyes.

6.

Make two holes in the clay for the fastening pin—to ensure a perfect fit, see *Getting Started*.

7.

Fire the shape on an oven-proof curved surface, such as a mug. When cool, paint with a coat of varnish. Cut a length of copper wire approximately 6 inches / 15.2 cm long. Gently curve the wire and carefully insert through both holes. Test it in your hair and trim the copper wire to the right length. File the tip smooth or cover with a tight fitting bead—pad the hole with a piece of rubber if it is loose. Finish by gluing the emerald crystal eyes in place.

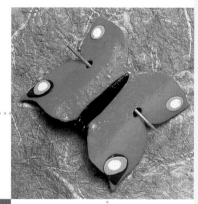

Variations on a Theme

Strips of different colored clays were pressed into the surface of this plain fish base. A coat of varnish intensifies the color and gives the barrette a glossy sheen (right).

A pretty butterfly is easy to cut from brightly-colored clay. The body and detail on the wing tips were added using separate pieces of clay (far right).

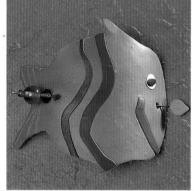

Acknowledgments

Grateful thanks to the many people without whose help and support this book would not have been published. First and most important, to my parents for their endless patience and for turning a blind eye when I used their home as a design studio. To Lindsey Stock and Jackie Schou for their additional design ideas, and to Paul Forrester for his creative photography. And, finally, to Shawna Mullen and Martha Wetherill, who made sense of everything I have written and gave valuable support and encouragement when times got tough.

About the Author

Jo Moody is a journalist who has spent many years working for women's magazines that specialize in fashion and crafts. She is now a freelance stylist and writer, contributing features and designs to a variety of publications. Her childhood fascination with jewelry has developed into a passion—she loves rediscovering traditional crafts and using them in new ways to transform everyday things into truly beautiful jewelry.